COLIN BELL – RELUCTANT HERO:
THE AUTOBIOGRAPHY OF
A MANCHESTER CITY AND ENGLAND LEGEND

Colin Bell played for Manchester City between 1966 and 1979, during which time he made just under 500 appearances and scored 152 goals. He still lives in Manchester.

Ian Cheeseman is a reporter for BBC Radio Manchester and has been a Manchester City fan all his life. He is forty-six years old and is married with two children. This is his first book.

COLIN BELL

RELUCTANT HERO

The Autobiography of a Manchester City
and England Legend

Colin Bell MBE with **Ian Cheeseman**
Foreword by Sir Bobby Charlton CBE

MAINSTREAM
PUBLISHING
EDINBURGH AND LONDON

For Marie, Dawn and Jon
(Colin Bell)

For Mum and Dad
Rosemarie and Tom
(Ian Cheeseman)

Reprinted, 2014
This edition, 2006

First published in Great Britain in 2005 by
MAINSTREAM PUBLISHING COMPANY
(EDINBURGH) LTD
7 Albany Street
Edinburgh EH1 3UG

ISBN 9781845960872

A catalogue record for this book is available
from the British Library

Printed and bound in Great Britain by Clays Ltd, Elcograf S.p.A.

Contents

Foreword

I hope City fans are not upset that an old Man United player is writing the foreword for one of their great heroes. I would have been very disappointed if I'd not had the opportunity. Colin Bell has been a great pal of mine but he's also one of *my* great heroes. I used to love watching him play because he comes from the same part of the world as me. We both, in our own ways, went to try and find our fame and fortune in football. I was always very aware of Colin Bell. I'm very proud that I've got the opportunity to say what I think of him and that people have got the chance to read about him.

Colin Bell was unquestionably a great player, and I don't use the word 'great' lightly. He was my kind of player. I used to read about him before I actually saw him play, which was when he was at Bury. I used to scan the papers every week to see how the local teams had done and I came to the conclusion that Colin Bell must be a good player because he seemed to be man of the match every week. Once I found out he came from the North-east, I followed his progress even more closely. It really upset me when City signed him.

He was a great athlete with a great football brain and a very dedicated person. He didn't need motivating; he did that himself. He had his own standards and you can't fail to be impressed by his playing record.

I got the opportunity to work with him occasionally when we were in the same squad for England and I was amazed by his strength and fitness. When a player with those assets has also got a football brain, and you ally that to pace and the other abilities he had, you have a really exceptional player. I was really disappointed we didn't get him at Old Trafford; sadly, I don't think there was ever a chance. I was always pleased when Colin did well – I'm sure the North-east was very proud of him.

He epitomised everything about that part of the country: people there work hard and play hard. It's tough in that area and to succeed you have to do something a bit special. Colin Bell did just that. He was probably undersold as a footballer at national level because he happened to burst onto the international scene just after England won the World Cup. At that time, the team almost picked itself, with the likes of Alan Ball and Martin Peters standing in Colin's way. I never felt he got the chance to show what he could do at international level. I think I only played two or three games with him; he often came on as a substitute at the time I was in the team.

I wish I could have started more games alongside Colin Bell but I had a great admiration for him as a player and as a person – and still have. He scored against us (United) on many occasions, which was always a hard pill to swallow! You can't ignore talent and he was an unbelievable talent. Had he played for England in an earlier era, or a little later, he would be a more world-renowned player – not just a player who stood out for one of the great club sides in England.

He was an outstanding player and it's been a huge privilege

and pleasure to watch him play with such great movement, grace, ability, stamina and flair. He scored his fair share of goals, too. I understand why he's rated as the best Manchester City player of all time and I would agree with that. I'm honoured to tell people my thoughts on Colin Bell and be part of a book that allows people to find out more about him.

Sir Bobby Charlton CBE

Introduction

I first met Colin Bell at a charity cricket match at Prestwich Heys. I was a small boy and he was the greatest footballer that had ever lived. I shook like a leaf as he signed the picture of him that I had carefully cut out of one of the football magazines. I idolised Colin because he was more than just a great player. He had a dignity, a modesty and even a shyness that made it easy for me to identify with him. That was back in the early 1970s.

More than three decades and a lifetime of experiences later, I got to know Colin through occasional appearances together at Manchester City supporters' functions. During the summer of 2002, the year Manchester staged the Commonwealth Games, I was offered the chance, through the BBC, to nominate someone to carry the baton on one leg of its pre-Games journey around the country. I nominated my hero, Colin Bell, because I knew he wouldn't be pushing himself forward to do such a thing.

He accepted my 'no strings attached' offer and quietly, and without any publicity, ran along Ashton Old Road near the City of Manchester Stadium on a sunny afternoon in July. He rang me a few days later to thank me for my part in setting up the opportunity and for fulfilling my promise not to put him in the media spotlight, which he is so determined to avoid.

We talked for about 20 minutes about his experiences as part of the Queen's Jubilee Baton Relay, Manchester City and lots of other things. Eventually, as the conversation concluded, he thanked me again, several times. I suggested that if he was so grateful he might want to grant me an exclusive radio interview. 'Not likely,' he replied, 'I'm not comfortable doing that sort of thing.' I countered with the suggestion that I might write his life story in a book. The rest, of course, is history.

During the last couple of years, I've spent many happy hours in the company of Colin, getting to know him and gaining his trust. On the journey up to Hesleden, the small village in County Durham where he grew up, we talked about anything and everything. I met his sister, saw the school he attended as a boy, visited the places he'd lived, played and learned his football. He wouldn't make himself known at his former school; he didn't want any fuss.

At one of his old clubs, Horden Colliery Welfare Juniors, we were refused access to their ground to take photographs, so I ended up taking one while both he and I were balanced precariously on ornamental rocks in the car park next to the main gate; that was after we'd both shinned up a drainpipe on one side of the stadium to get a better view! When I'd requested access, their officials told us we had to put our request in writing to the 'committee'. Colin stood quietly behind me as I tried to convince them to make an exception for a true sporting legend. We failed, because to some people rules are rules!

It was a daunting prospect to write the story of the most idolised player in Manchester City's history. I was honoured to have the task of spending my 'day job' commentating on my team home and away for BBC radio, and spending much of my free time in the company of, or writing about, the greatest player to have played football.

The biggest potential problem was that I might not like him. The image I had built up of him from watching him play, reading about him and from his rare public appearances, was of someone who was special both on and off a football pitch. Someone who had never forgotten his roots and was still very grounded, despite the relative riches he had enjoyed as a professional footballer. The more I got to know him, the more I realised I had nothing to fear. The word 'great' is overused but in Colin's case I can truly say he is a great man, as well as being a great footballer.

Once he drops his guard, he is funny, entertaining and totally sincere. To some, he might seem distant or even aloof but that's just his shyness. Even now he seems amazed that he's still remembered so fondly and feels awkward in the public spotlight. As a youngster, he'd cross the road to avoid being recognised; these days he'll blend into the background at every opportunity.

In more intimate surroundings, he starts to open up and once he gets going he's hard to stop; not that you'd want to stop him. He talks passionately about the sport he loves, and cares as deeply about the Manchester City of the new millennium as he did about the team during his glory days.

As a player, Colin had the rare ability to be flamboyant and yet industrious. He was a natural athlete who was graceful on the ball but fiercely tenacious without it. He could pass short or long and split defences with laser-like precision passes but he was equally able to tackle and play his part in breaking down the opposition. He'd often win the ball on the edge of his own penalty area before driving powerfully to the other end of the pitch to finish off the move he started.

His basic skills of passing and trapping the ball with either foot, though he was naturally right-footed, were perfect. Most people associate Colin with the nickname 'Nijinsky', given to him by the City coach Malcolm Allison. The comparison was with the supreme fitness and stamina of the great racehorse, which won the triple crown of the 2,000 Guineas, the Epsom Derby and the St Leger. The horse got its name from the Russian ballet dancer. Colin's nickname is totally appropriate in both cases, for he also showed great balance, style and elegance in everything he did on a football pitch.

Colin signed for Manchester City in 1966 and during his 13 years at the club he helped the Blues win the League Championship, FA Cup and League Cup as well as the European Cup-Winners' Cup. He made 492 appearances for City, including 3 as a substitute, scoring 152 goals. He made 48 appearances for England. It would have been many more but for a terrible knee injury at the age of just 29 from which he never fully recovered.

The list of people happy to sing Colin's praises is endless. Naturally, his former City teammates hold him in high esteem. Goalkeeper Joe Corrigan is typical when he describes Colin by saying, 'He had everything. It's one of the biggest tragedies of English football that he got injured so early whilst at the pinnacle of his career and that we never saw the continuation of the best of Colin Bell. I think he would have been a natural leader and captain of England for a very long time.'

Off the field, Joe describes Colin as, 'A great fella. There was nothing fancy about him, he just got on with his job and was a great role model. If kids could get videos that show his commitment in games and the runs he used to make, they'd learn a lot.'

During his two-year battle to get fit again, physiotherapist

Freddie Griffiths spent many hours with Colin and sums him up by saying, 'Colin was the perfect footballer. He is a very private man, with great principles and dignity. He is a man you would love to have as a brother and a friend. He is very genuine to anyone he thinks is deserving of his respect. He has always set himself very high social, moral and physical standards. It's no coincidence that his closer friends in the City team were the honest, fair, upright and hard-working lads.'

Freddie illustrates one of Colin's great strengths, his determination to be part of a successful team, with this story: 'I asked him, "With your pace, strength and skill, if you got the ball on the halfway line and there was a big strong lumbering centre-half in between you and the goal, what would you do?" Colin's answer was that he'd draw the man towards him and wait for a teammate to come in support, before laying the ball into their path so they could score. When I asked why he wouldn't take the man on, his reply was, "It would create a potential weakness and being part of a successful team is better than personal glory."'

Perhaps the reason so many opponents feared Colin was that he rarely took the wrong option.

Kevin Keegan played alongside Colin for England but usually competed against him at club level. The former Liverpool striker admits to being 'a big admirer of Mike Doyle, Tony Book and the rest of the players from City's glory days in the 1960s and '70s. Colin had it all, though, that's why I think he's been the club's best player of the century. Other players might have been able to match his running but not his skill. Some might have matched his ability but not his strength or football brain; he was a clever player, too.'

Former West Ham United and England player Geoff Hurst told me, 'The Bell, Lee, Summerbee era was great for

Manchester City. You tended to look at Colin and say he was very fit. People called him Nijinsky because he was strong and could get up and down the pitch. That was what you focused on initially but later in life I realised more and more that he had many other assets. I played with Colin for England towards the end of my career and it was then that I fully appreciated his great ability. Today, Colin Bell would be a great player – and worth a few bob, too!'

One of Maine Road's greatest games took place in December 1967, when Tottenham Hotspur were City's opponents for the so-called 'ballet on ice'. The great Alan Mullery was in the Spurs side that day and pays Colin this tribute: 'The easiest accolade I can give him is that he lived up to his nickname fully. I always remember our manager at Tottenham, Bill Nicholson, saying after a game against City that he should have signed him from Bury. When we asked him why he'd failed, he told us that Colin had preferred to go to Manchester City. City's gain was definitely Tottenham's loss. He'd still be a star in today's football and he would fit into any team.'

The great Tom Finney didn't play against Colin, his time as a player had long since ended, but as a journalist he watched him play on many occasions. 'I was actually with the *News of the World* when I was watching him at City. He played many, many outstanding games. City was a big club then with Francis Lee and Mike Summerbee, those sorts of players. I think Colin Bell was as good as anything I've ever seen. His speciality was being a great passer of the ball and he was a very good finisher, but above all a good passer.'

Although I could have written a book that consisted entirely of tributes to Colin, from the great and the good, I've found space for just one more. The former Everton and Nottingham Forest striker, Duncan McKenzie, remembers playing against

Colin at club level and with him on the international stage. 'I played with him for England when Joe Mercer was in charge. We went on a tour of Eastern Europe together. "Belly" was a brick, an absolute brick.

'Colin was perpetual motion but he also had unbelievable skill. He was good in the air, which people don't really talk about. He had fabulous close control with some wonderful little touches and great vision. I'm sure he would have played for England a hundred times. He would have stood shoulder to shoulder with the great players of today. Belly was a player for today, then!'

During the process of writing this book, I have concluded that Colin hasn't got a particularly good memory; still, you can't have everything! You would be amazed how many times I proved Colin remembered a sequence of events in the wrong order.

It's been a long process with a few ups and downs along the way but, as with most things in life, you don't achieve things without hard work and the support of your friends and family. I would, therefore, like to place on record my thanks to my friend and inspiration Fred Eyre.

Fred is a fellow broadcaster and author with whom I have worked together on many occasions. I have learnt a lot from him and he has always been prepared to give me advice and support when I've doubted myself. Thanks, Fred.

Manchester City's historian, Gary James, and his counterpart at Bury, Gordon Sorfleet, have been a great help, along with countless other people at various clubs which have some connection to Colin's career. All of Colin's former teammates and opponents have been very generous with their time, including Colin's hero Bobby Charlton, who treated me to a wonderful breakfast as we discussed his foreword to this book. Thanks also to Dennis Chapman for his help with the statistics section.

Naturally, I would like to thank my wife, Irene, and my children, Steven and Daniel, for allowing me the time I've needed to research and work on this book, and my friends, particularly my City 'soul mate' Charlie, for their encouragement.

Most of all, I'd like to thank Colin's wife, Marie, who made me feel welcome at the family home from day one, and to the whole Bell family, particularly Colin's son Jon, for their sincerity and for believing in me. None of this would have been possible without the sublime skills Colin provided on the football pitch and I now admire him even more than I did before I truly knew him as a person. Thanks for trusting me with such an important project.

Colin Bell is one of the most modest people I've ever met, in a world where being an 'in yer face celebrity' seems to convince the masses that mediocrity is to be celebrated. As you read Colin's story, I'm sure you'll agree – even if you didn't see him play – that he is one of life's true superstars; but that's with a small 's', because that's the way he would want it.

Ian Cheeseman

CHAPTER ONE

Growing Up in the North-east

By most people's definition of a normal childhood, I didn't have one. It wasn't until many years after my birth that I realised my 'mum' was actually my aunt and that my actual mother had died soon after my first birthday. I have no memory of her, just a few pictures passed on through the family.

Even when I found out the truth about those early years of my life, I believed for many years that my mother had been taken ill during child birth and never recovered. Part of the reason for writing this book was to learn more of the details of my youth that I'd never previously enquired about. I'm not sure why I'd been reluctant to ask about those early days before.

I returned to Hesleden, the village of my birth, as part of my voyage of discovery so I could talk to my older sister, Eileen, who helped fill in some of the blanks that had existed for so long. Although I've talked to my sister many times before, the process of writing the book meant that I could hear the full story from her. I relished the chance to hear the answers to questions I'd held back from asking.

I was born at home, as was the norm in those days, in Hesleden, County Durham. It was a normal birth with my father beside himself with glee because I was a boy. He'd wanted a boy when my older sister Eileen was born but when I came into the world on 26 February 1946 his wish was realised. At that moment, as he held me for the first time, he was probably already hoping to see me play football for England.

After a few months together as a 'normal' family, my mother was taken ill and I moved in with my aunt, Ella (Dixon), because my father couldn't really cope with being a single parent. My father, John William Bell, worked at Blackhall Colliery, a coal mine quite close to where we lived, within sight of Hartlepool, about halfway between Sunderland and Middlesbrough. My father's long and unsocial shift-work didn't seem to fit with the requirements of being a single parent to a young girl and small boy, so after much soul searching he decided it would be in everyone's interests if Aunt Ella took on the role of our substitute mother.

My sister Eileen moved in with Aunt Ella at the same time as I did. Eileen is 12 years older than me, so has a much clearer recollection of our early life together. I'd always thought I'd gone straight to Aunt Ella's after I was born but it seems I didn't. My mother, Elizabeth, gave birth to me in the February and was still at home for my first birthday.

It was just after her 39th birthday, on 2 April 1947, that she went into hospital with a complaint referred to at the time as a 'growth of the back body'. We know it today as bowel cancer and if she'd been ill now, it would probably have been curable. However, despite numerous operations, she died in the August. They'd tried everything to save her, including a few treatments that were experimental at the time.

No one in the family realised the seriousness of the illness until the end. They always believed she would recover. She didn't seem to be very poorly and could walk around. They didn't take me into hospital very often because I was just a baby and my mother would get upset because I didn't recognise her. When I did go in, apparently I'd run up and down the ward, when all she wanted to do was get hold of me and give me a cuddle. I'm told I was very quick to walk and that by ten months I was already running around and causing all sorts of trouble.

'Mum' (Aunt Ella) had three older children of her own by the time Eileen and I went to live with her. The oldest, Harry, had left home but Joyce, who was 20, and Walter, two years older at 22, were still both living there. Dad was 42 years old and from having three of us in the house, my mother, Eileen and me, suddenly he was alone. It must have been a difficult time for him. He'd always wanted a son, so I was the apple of his eye.

Dad was a pretty good footballer, playing for Hesleden Rising Star, who twice played in the Durham Amateur Cup final. The village was emptied when there was a football match on in those days. The crowd would be two or three deep around the side of the pitch. My sister Eileen tells me that Dad was an excellent player – and it seems all the Bells were. Uncle Jim, Dad, Uncle Chuck and Uncle Kit were all good players. Eileen even played a bit too at the age of about 15. Her biggest asset was her speed.

Dad was an inside-forward, as I was to become. He used to hang in the air for the crosses that came from Uncle Jim and as a result his nickname was 'Jumper'. Eileen didn't see him play much because he was nearly 30 when she was born. Nottingham Forest and another club came looking at Dad but he was too old by the time they spotted him and it was too late for him to take up football as a professional career.

Our mother had been a footballer, too. She played during the

1926 General Strike to help raise funds for the poorer people in the village. The crowds for those games would have been bigger than you get in the lower divisions today. She'd always be playing football with the lads around the village. She was very strong and athletic and good at sports, though she wasn't very tall.

I'm told that the first thing my mother said when she saw me was, 'Dad has got his little footballer after all.' Eileen says it broke her heart, years later, when they played 'Abide with Me' at the 1969 FA Cup final, because they'd played that at our mother's funeral. If she'd lived to see me play at Wembley that day, I'm sure she would have been as proud as a peacock.

I lived with Mum (Aunt Ella) and Eileen in the seaside town of Blackhall Rocks at 9 Hart Street, and went to school in Hesleden, about two or three miles away. Although I was aware of my dad, I didn't see him very often. I lived with my mum in quite an isolated way, a life that didn't really include my dad. Although there was a bus between the villages every half hour or so, life wasn't like it is now with people visiting each other all the time and of course no one had cars. I can't remember seeing him a lot while I was a small boy, although we would bump into him from time to time.

To be honest, there were lots of times in those early years when Mum wasn't there either. She used to work as a cleaner at the National Coal Board offices at Castle Eden, a few miles away. She needed to work to support us and would come home at nine o'clock, after it had gone dark. When she came, I'd be kicking a ball around under the nearby street lamp. It was like a floodlit pitch.

Typically, as she got home, she'd shout, 'Come on, son, come on, Col,' as she approached me. I'd follow her in and she'd make tea. That was my lifestyle in those early years. I knew nothing different. I was a loner, spending hours on that street corner playing football on my own.

Eileen used to take me to school with her now and again, even though I was still below school age myself. Eileen says she had no choice. 'If Mum was busy with a hospital appointment or something else important, I would ask the teacher, Jackson, if it was OK to bring Colin in. I told him I'd have to stay off school if he didn't let me. To start with, Colin would sit next to me in class, drawing, crayoning or something like that. Later, they'd let him go into the schoolyard and give him a ball. Once he was out there, which was usually later in the day, most of the lessons would be disrupted because everybody would be watching him kick the ball around through the huge windows.

'In some ways, I felt more like Colin's mother than his older sister, because of the role I played at that time. I was very protective of him. I think it was because I was old enough to appreciate the effect our mother dying had on him. I was hurt, too, so I decided I would be like his mother and not let anybody hurt *him*.'

Despite not having my 'real' mum around, I had a very happy childhood. Mum looked after me and cared for me during the early years of my life and I loved her. I didn't call her 'Aunt Ella'; I called her 'Mum'. As far as I was concerned, she was my mum. Eileen stayed with Aunt Ella and me for two years, until she left school at the age of fifteen. She then returned to live with our dad now that she was more able to help out around the home and look after him.

At the age of seven, my life suddenly felt like it had been turned upside down. It was a dark evening in November 1953. It sticks vividly in my mind. Mum and Dad were with me at the top of the street where he lived in Hesleden. I can't really remember how we got there; it didn't seem significant at the time. I noticed that Dad was tugging on one of my arms and Mum was pulling on the other wrist. Both of them were saying that they wanted me. I started crying. I wanted to go with my mum because I'd lived with her all my life. My mum was in tears.

I don't know whether they'd organised this meeting or whether it was just a spur-of-the-moment thing. My father insisted I was going with him. I was going back home in his eyes, although I had no memories of living with him. Eileen had heard Dad and Aunt Ella planning the meeting and says she could foresee the heartache that lay ahead.

'Dad asked Aunt Ella to meet him with Colin, as he left The Hardwick pub, so he could take him home. She was very reluctant and didn't want to part with him. It was very hard for my dad as well. I think they all came up to the square at the end of Single Burdon Street and Double Burdon Street and the dispute happened there.'

My father got his way that day and the three of us, Eileen, Dad and me, were reunited in Hesleden. Being only seven years old, I accepted the change quickly, although I was probably upset for a month or two. I can't really remember now but it's amazing how, after a while, kids being kids, you get over things. I'll never forget that night, though, when I was in the middle of a tug-of-war for who should have me.

Eileen had met the love of her life, Bart, while back home with Dad and at the age of 19, she married him. The pair started their life together living with Dad in Single Burdon Street. This had provided the solution to his childcare problems. Eileen and Bart were willing and able to look after me while he was working down the pit.

Our house was on a street among half a dozen parallel streets that ran down a hill away from Hesleden Village Church towards a stream. It was a short walk to Hesleden School. We called the wooded area down by the stream 'the dean' and the nearby hill was known locally as 'Charlie's Bank'. I spent many happy hours sliding down that hill on a piece of old cardboard and rolling eggs down at Easter.

The house we lived in wasn't the biggest: a two up-two down mid-terrace with an outside toilet and coal shed. The backyard also provided a location for the boiler, which supplied the hot water for washing our clothes, and the tin bath, which was used in front of the open fire. There was a piano in the downstairs room. No one played it, but it was there.

The house wasn't very big, so Eileen and Bart shared one bedroom while I slept with my dad. That was the arrangement until Eileen and Bart's son, Keith, who was born within a year of their marriage, was four years old.

Although my father was a miner, the closest I came to going down a pit myself was seeing him come off his shift. The miners would come up in the cage covered in coal dust, wearing their pit helmets. The whites of their eyes glared out from their dirty faces. I would think 80 per cent of the men in the village were miners, so it seemed the natural thing for most boys to do when they left school. I'm not sure my father realistically knew what he had in mind for *me* at that stage but he certainly didn't want me to become a miner.

Life in Hesleden was simple and money wasn't plentiful. I've got to admit that schoolwork was not my number one priority. My schooling was basic. I can't remember being given much homework – perhaps a couple of maths problems or a few bits of English now and again but nothing serious. I only went to school because it was expected and everybody else did. We all went through the process simply because it was the thing to do.

It seems hard to believe these days but there was only one car in the village when I was a boy. We used to walk down to wherever it was parked and just look at it. We didn't have a television when I was very young; in fact, it was a big highlight of my childhood when we got our first black-and-white TV.

I used to love watching *The Adventures of William Tell* with Conrad Phillips as William and Willoughby Goddard as the dastardly Gessler. Even bath time wasn't like it is now. We used to have one bath a week in front of the open fire. That old tin bath was filled by bringing hot water in from the kitchen, one kettle at a time.

I used to get sent on errands and I'd always take a tennis ball with me. I'd have the piece of paper in my hand that told me what I had to get from the shops in the village and the tennis ball at my feet. I'd dribble the ball from home to the shop, trapping it as it came back off the wall or slowly rolling it up the path.

I didn't need pals to practise my skills because keeping the ball up or playing against the wall in the backyard was enough for me. Occasionally, when my nephew Keith was a bit older, I used to stick him in goal on the green in front of the house. There was a post there and I used to put a coat down and practise shooting against him. Generally, though, it was just me.

As a child the football team I watched most was Hartlepool United, simply because it was the easiest ground to get to. I did manage a few trips to Sunderland's Roker Park, though, and that was where I really wanted to go. My early football hero was Len Shackleton.

As a Sunderland supporter it had to be Shack. I saw him play a few times. He was an eye-catcher. On the ball he used to do little tricks and legend has it that in one game he actually took the ball to the corner flag and sat on it. I wish I'd been at that game.

He was an individual rather than a team player. I didn't really understand the game properly back then but he caught my eye, a bit like Rodney Marsh during his time at Manchester City in the 1970s. I never used to try to be like Shack though. People have always asked me if I copied anyone else but the answer is that I just wanted to be me.

Another hero of mine was Charlie Hurley, who came along after Shack. He was a big, dominant centre-back. I actually played against him during my time at City in September 1968. He was still with Sunderland, towards the end of his playing career. As I recall, the Roker Park crowd had been singing 'King Charlie' when Mike Summerbee, our centre-forward that day, out-jumped him to score a goal. We won the game 4–0. He'll always be King Charlie to me.

It used to take me an hour to travel to Roker Park, using three different buses. I probably only saw Len Shackleton play 20 times because it was so difficult to get there. I wish I could have seen him more but I was the only member of the family who wanted to go. My dad had gone past the stage where he wanted to watch football matches and my sister was always too busy.

Every Christmas I used to be given the same presents: a Sunderland shirt, football boots, shin pads, shorts, socks and a ball. In truth, that's all I wanted and all I needed. I do remember receiving a green racing bike one year. It was second-hand of course. The lad a few doors down had grown too big for it but I was delighted to get it.

Despite getting the same presents every year, I used to get excited about Father Christmas coming along, just like everyone else. The bedroom I shared with my father had a door that opened inwards, so I had to manoeuvre around to my father's side of the bed, to exit the room.

On Christmas morning, with my father fast asleep next to me, I would creep, an inch at a time, towards the door. Just as I finally got there I'd hear, 'Hey, get yourself back into bed, lad, he's not been yet.' It might have taken me an hour and a half to reach that far and all for nothing!

I had total respect for my dad, though I don't think we were as close or as friendly as we could have been. I was frightened of him at times. He used to rule with an iron fist. If I was up late I'd be in trouble. I used to enjoy watching the big European football matches on TV, but they'd go on past nine o'clock and that was past my bedtime. My dad would sit in the kitchen and I'd be in the front room watching the game. When it came to bedtime he'd simply shout, 'Hey, lad, bedtime.'

My sister would always stick up for me because she knew I loved the football and there'd sometimes be a bit of a tiff. I used to sit there keeping quiet while they argued it out. There was never a physical threat from my dad. He'd never lift his hand to smack me. He simply had a strong, commanding voice.

My dad was a perfectionist in many ways. As far as his personal hygiene and appearance was concerned, everything had to be just right. Every weekend, he'd clean everyone's shoes, going through them with the polish until they were perfect. He'd also make sure that his hair was just right, even though he only had a couple of strands on top. He'd part them and dab on a bit of Vaseline. He was always immaculate.

My dad lived in a man's world. He spent a lot of his time down the mine or in the pub with his mates. It was a hard physical life. He'd been down the mine from the age of 12 and was adamant that I would never follow in his footsteps.

A great deal of my youth was spent honing my football skills. I'd practise in the backyard at home for hours on end. I would kick the ball onto the slope of the roof, heading it against the wall when it came down. My dad would bring home blocks of wood from the colliery to make into sticks for the fire. I'd line them up in the yard and dribble around them.

I often played alongside older boys in the school team and was also selected for Durham representative games. I was only 11 when I played for the East Durham Under-15s.

As far as I was aware, my dad didn't come and watch me play during those schoolboy days, although my sister Eileen says that dad *was* there on many occasions – but he kept discreetly in the background.

'Dad would go over with us to watch Colin play but he didn't want Colin to know he was there. He'd often pull his collar up and stand away from us, so that Colin wouldn't notice him. He wouldn't say much, just quietly watch the game. If Colin miskicked, missed a tackle or made a mistake during the match he'd just mutter "Oh, Colin" under his breath and that would be it.

'Our dad was very, very proud of Colin. Sometimes, as he became better known for his football abilities, the local kids would be on the street outside our house shouting, "Colin Bell, Colin Bell", and Dad thought that was lovely. He never looked for reflected glory, though. He just wanted to be in the background. My dad and Colin didn't spend as much time together as they might have done because of Dad working shifts but they did play dominoes and other games like that together whenever they could.'

I suppose I was good at most sports from an early age. One of the teachers at school noticed my abilities as soon as he came to Hesleden. Brian Jemmett was principally a class teacher but his enthusiasm for sport meant that it wasn't very long before he was giving up his spare time to organise athletics and football. However, he says it took a while to find a group of youngsters who shared his enthusiasm.

'The first group of lads I had for sport were dreadful. They used to turn up for football wearing big boots and flat caps. When I first came across Colin, he was only about nine years old but I could see his potential right away. He was only small but good enough to keep out of bother. By the time he was 11, he was playing in the first team, mixing with the 15 year olds.

'He wasn't a prima donna but he knew he was a good player. He never moaned at the other kids who weren't as good. It was only a small school but eventually we had a good bunch of lads with about six standing out above the rest.

'Colin used to help me out with all sorts of things, marking the pitch lines and even digging the long-jump pit one year. I taught them to swim in the open-air baths down at Horden, though even to this day Colin doesn't enjoy swimming or do it very well. In the winter, we had to chip the ice off the surface so they could climb in.

'I could tell from very early on that Colin had the talent to make it as a professional footballer, so I used to make him wear a plimsoll on his right foot to make him develop his left. I used to make him play inside-left. He was a kid who had a good eye for any ball and he could have been very good at cricket or tennis.'

My cricketing abilities were also developed in the backyard at home, with the help of Eileen's son, Keith, who is eight years younger than me. We grew up together as brothers and spent many hours playing football and cricket together. We used to play in our backyard using the dustbin as a wicket. I was always Middlesex and Keith was Lancashire. Eileen used to watch us through the kitchen window. Keith was forever running in and out of the gate getting the ball back as I hit it all over the place.

Eileen would come outside and tell me to let Keith have a turn at batting but I said he'd only have his turn when he got me out. Eileen would *make* me let Keith have a bat but as soon as she got back in the house I'd have got him out and I'd be batting again. Eileen says the other downside of us playing cricket in the backyard was the breakages.

'Every now and again there would be the tinkling sound of breaking glass. I used to ring my husband Bart, who worked at the nearby brewery, and after a while he wouldn't even ask what had happened. He knew the measurements of the windows by heart and would bring a new piece of glass home with him. I don't think the putty ever hardened around some of those windows.'

My teacher, Brian Jemmett, took me for a cricket trial. I can remember being faced with an old selector, puffing away on a cigarette, his waistcoat wrinkled up, covered in grey ash. I don't think he ever looked up as I played in that game. I never had a chance. It was the old boys' network. As a result, I never really achieved anything at cricket during my schooldays. Brian Jemmett took me for sport until the age of 14 and there is no doubt that he played a crucial part in my development.

I failed the exams I took at the age of 11 for the A.J. Dawson Grammar School in Wellfield. I had no interest in passing examinations and going to a grammar school; it just didn't seem that it would make a huge difference to my life, so I wasn't particularly disappointed. It's different these days, of course, but back then all I could think of was becoming a professional footballer.

I always had the belief that I could achieve my dream – and eventually that was what happened – but I've seen thousands of kids through the years who've believed the same as I did and sacrificed their education for a life of football, only to fall by the wayside. Now that I am older and wiser, I realise that just because it worked out for me not all young players will be so lucky.

As I grew older, I took more interest in my education and at the age of 15 I went to the Technical College in Stockton. I often rode down to Mum's on my bike and then travelled on through Hartlepool to Stockton by bus. I'd call in again on my way home and she'd make me wonderful suet puddings that simmered over the fire.

She used to boil them in cloths, tied with string, and made them with apple or jam. I loved them. They were like desserts but I had them as the main course. She used to make fresh bread, 'stotty cake' and other things. The smells in Mum's house can't be described. No wonder I'd always have my tea there before I cycled home again.

Being more aware of the need to have a good academic education, by now I was starting to achieve some modest successes. I passed a few exams on the engineering side, though I can't prove that I was awarded those qualifications because I never bothered picking up the certificates. Perhaps they've still got them somewhere in a brown envelope, waiting for me to collect them. The trouble was that my college studies were running hand-in-hand with my football trials for various different football clubs in the area.

Among the teams I played for at that time was the Technical College. We played our games in Billingham on Wednesdays. I used to play in goal for them because I got fed up with playing in the same position I played at the weekend. I remember making a great save on one of those occasions. I was just outside the penalty area and somebody tried to lob me. I had to run back to the penalty spot, diving backwards towards my own goal and managed to palm it over the crossbar. It was one of the best saves I ever made.

One of our teachers, Mr Dee, did some scouting for Sheffield Wednesday and I remember him asking me one week if I fancied a trial at Hillsborough as a goalkeeper. He didn't realise that I was really an outfield player as he'd only ever seen me play in goal but I didn't fancy being a goalkeeper every week – just occasionally, for a bit of fun.

CHAPTER TWO
Turning Professional

By the age of 14 or 15, I was starting to get noticed outside the village and immediate area. I had been playing for the school team, often with boys much older than me, and for East Durham and Billingham Technical College. The best junior team in the region at that time was Horden Colliery Welfare Juniors, who scoured the area for the best young players. The Wright brothers, who ran Horden Juniors, visited us at home to ask if I would play for them.

I agreed and started making the trip to Horden, which is about four or five miles up the coastline from Blackhall Rocks, on a regular basis. We used to win games very easily; in fact, I remember winning one game 21–1! I don't know what went wrong for the goal we conceded. We were definitely the best players in the area. I had some great times at Horden Juniors and it was the place where I first came to the attention of scouts from the professional clubs.

There were representatives from football league clubs at every home game and most of the lads in the team had trials at different places. A few different clubs were interested in me, though Newcastle were the first who really made a move. I was asked to play in their 'End' side. The trial game took place on a pitch close to St James's Park.

As time went by, other clubs also showed an interest in signing me, with Arsenal, Wolves, Hull City, Bury and Huddersfield Town among those who made enquiries. I actually went for further discussions with Huddersfield, Bury and Arsenal.

I didn't do myself justice during my trial at Arsenal because I'd injured my back at school in the preceding days. My doctor told me I had a sprain. I didn't tell my dad about the problem because I was frightened he would stop me going. I was worried that I'd miss the chance and wouldn't get another. I managed to successfully hide any signs of the injury from Dad as we went down to London a few days later.

It was quite an experience for my dad and me to visit the capital. We stayed in a place quite close to the main stadium in Highbury. The training grounds, which were beautiful, were about 20 miles outside London. Highbury was pretty impressive, too. We'd never seen anything like it. They had a commissionaire on the door and once you moved inside you passed through a marble entrance hall, filled with mementoes of past successes and sculptures of those who'd been their great heroes. It was very grand. We didn't see things like that where I lived. We didn't go very far inside after that, the whole thing being a bit of a culture shock.

There were hundreds of lads at those trials, with seven or eight games taking place simultaneously. I remember afterwards, when all the parents and kids gathered together, the Arsenal manager, Billy Wright, got up and spoke. Just to see him standing there in front of us filled us with awe.

This was Billy Wright! He told us he had selected a few lads and thanked everyone for trying so hard and travelling so far to take part in the trials. As I hadn't been told I'd been successful, I assumed I wouldn't be joining Arsenal.

I received the rejection letter a few days later. If I'd been a bit older, the words within that letter might have affected me but to be honest at that age it just went over my head. I've still got the letter, the second paragraph of which reads:

> I hope you enjoyed playing in this trial. We for our part felt it was of a very fair standard and although in our opinion you did not come up to our requirements, this does not mean there may not be a place for you in professional football with another club whose standards are not quite as high as those at which we are aiming.

The letter was signed by Billy Wright.

I didn't allow that rejection to affect my self-confidence; I knew I was a decent player and I still believed in my ability. Soon after returning from London I went to the doctor again and he told me to rest for a month.

Once I'd fully recovered, I was back playing two or three times a week. Horden Juniors continued to dominate the area, qualifying for the amateur cup final. Naturally, there were scouts from lots of different clubs at the game, including Heppell Hodgson, the Arsenal scout, who ironically tipped off his Bury counterpart, Ron Batty (who'd played full-back for Newcastle) that I was the player to look at.

Huddersfield Town and Bury both asked if I would talk to them. My dad and I went to Huddersfield first. It was too far to go there and back in a day, so we stopped overnight. We went to the pictures that evening to see *Summer Holiday* with Cliff

Richard. It was in colour and that was a treat for us. We'd never seen anything like it and Dad, in particular, was amazed.

By the time we arrived at the football ground to talk about my future, we were already impressed, but I never allowed Dad's excitement to affect my decision. The people at Huddersfield were very hospitable and exchanged pleasantries with me, passing the time of day, but they didn't really chat to me. I felt that something was missing and that was important to me. The friendly edge just wasn't there.

My experience at Bury was completely different. I went there for a week to play in two practice games. As it turned out, they wanted me to play for their reserves rather than play in training-ground matches. Playing in their reserve side was quite an experience. I played against Wolves and Everton.

In goal for Wolves was Malcolm Finlayson, who'd appeared in European competition for them, and their regular centre-half, England international Bill Slater, was also in the side. Billy Bingham was playing for Everton, so the opposition was impressive. I was only 17 years old so it was quite a challenge but I must have impressed the people at Bury, because they couldn't wait to sign me.

I'd really enjoyed myself during my brief time in Bury. On the final evening, before returning home to Hesleden, two of the club's directors came to the hotel to see my father and me. Everyone seemed very genuine and I felt like they were really interested in me, in a way I hadn't felt at Huddersfield. The truth is I'd already made my decision that Bury was the club for me by then but we still chatted to the Bury directors until three in the morning without agreeing anything.

I wanted to be fair to Huddersfield and felt the right thing to do was return home and think about it for a day or two before making a final decision. I've always believed in fairness and that seemed the right thing to do. Bury kept pushing me for a decision and I wanted to say yes but I felt it was more important to make the decision carefully than rush into it.

I went home and waited for a week or so before telling Bury that I would sign for them. Money was never a factor in the decision, both clubs having offered me £12 a week, but if Bury had only offered half that amount I would still have signed for them. I'm quite shy in many ways, so I needed to go somewhere where I felt at home. That was why I chose Bury.

Wolves did make a late attempt to persuade me to sign for them. They'd been impressed by the way I'd played for Bury against their reserve side. One of their scouts came to our house after first losing his way and turning up in Cold Hesleden, which is further up the coast near Sunderland. It was a snowy, freezing night and my sister Eileen says their scout brought a letter with him from the Wolves manager, Stan Cullis. It apparently said they must sign me urgently.

Arsenal and Newcastle had also shown some interest again, with the Arsenal scout saying he couldn't understand what had gone wrong during my trial down at Highbury. I wasn't interested, though. As far as I was concerned, these clubs were only coming back because they'd heard of other interest in me. My choice was to join Bury: they were the club for me.

I officially signed for Bury on 16 July 1963, having provisionally agreed terms a couple of months before. As part of my signing-on fee, the family got four tickets to the FA Cup final. It was Manchester United against Leicester City. Eileen went with us that day and I think she thought going to the cup final was better than getting a cash signing-on fee. We stood at the tunnel end and saw United win 3–1.

I made eighty-two league appearances for Bury during my three seasons with them. It proved to be a great grounding and

Bury was such a friendly club. Bob Stokoe was the manager when I joined them, though Bert Head was in charge by the time I left three years later.

Bob was a lovely person and a very good manager. He didn't have any money to spend on new players, so he spent his time working with the players he had. That worked out fine, because it meant there was no pressure on me and he was able to give me advice and help me continue to develop my skills and become more mature.

Bob was a bit of a Jekyll and Hyde character. Off the field, you couldn't find anyone nicer but he could be grumpy if things didn't go well on the pitch. He was a bad loser, like me.

I started off playing in the reserve side hoping to get my break in the first team. I remember playing against a Leeds United team at Elland Road that included the future England left-back, Terry Cooper. Terry kicked the ball into my face at one point and it left me with blood pouring from my nose onto my shirt.

On came our trainer, former England international Johnny Wheeler, who used to be at Liverpool. I asked him for some cotton wool to stuff up my nose and he, in return, asked me if my nose was normally underneath my right eye! I didn't know what he meant until I saw my reflection in the glass window of the medical room, just up the tunnel. What a sight – I looked like Frankenstein on a bad night!

A few days later, they took me to Bury General Hospital to try to sort my nose out. It was decided that I would need an operation, which took place a couple of weeks later. I'll never forget the doctor stuffing so many bandages up my nose that I wondered if they were going to start popping out of my mouth. It made me think of those magicians who pull flowers out of strange places!

During the summer that year, I walked past a freshly cut

privet hedge and inhaled a nose full of dust. I'd never suffered from hay fever but suddenly my eyes were streaming, my nose was running and I couldn't breathe. I've suffered from hay fever whenever the weather is dry ever since. I'm not sure if a broken nose can make you more susceptible to the problem but I blame Terry Cooper when my nose starts to run in midsummer!

I didn't play many games for Bury's reserves before breaking into the first team. My senior debut, ironically, was against Manchester City, at Maine Road, in February 1964. I think City had expected an easy win because we were such a small club compared to them. They didn't have it all their own way, though, and I scored the goal that gave us the lead.

It was at the North Stand end and I remember being through on goal with just Harry Dowd to beat. City were hoping I was offside but I kept my nerve, rounded Harry and slotted it in from the angle. It gave me a real boost scoring that goal and I lived on it for quite a while.

There were no substitutes in those days and Harry damaged his shoulder later in the game. I think he ended up with his arm in a sling but he had to carry on playing. He couldn't stay in goal, so they put him up front as a striker. He caused us all sorts of problems, running around all over the place. He caused more panic in our defence than their normal strikers had done, scoring the equaliser, which took the shine off things from my point of view.

I was settling in well at Bury and lived in digs in Park Hills Road, a ten-minute walk from Gigg Lane. I lived there with Mr and Mrs Platt for a couple of years and although I was homesick from time to time, I was generally very happy. My family never asked me if I was homesick and they never asked me to go back home, which allowed me to get on with being a professional footballer. It would have been the biggest mistake of my life if

I'd returned to Hesleden at that stage and, apart from the odd visit home, I never did.

More often than not, we trained on lower Gigg, which is about 400 yards down the road from Bury's stadium on Gigg Lane, down past the cemetery. We did occasionally play a practice match on the main pitch in the stadium but not often. On some days, we actually trained on the car park outside the ground, especially if we were doing a running session.

Sometimes we'd do sessions which involved running around those heavy medicine balls, or picking them up and using them as weights. Most of the work we were doing was designed to improve strength and stamina. I did sometimes get a little bored because the weeks often followed the same pattern. It became very predictable at times.

There were plenty of good players at the club while I was there. Gordon Atherton, Brian Turner, Brian Eastham, Colin Waldron and Chris Harker in goal, just to name a few. I'd seen Chris play a couple of years earlier in a game at Sunderland. Chris was involved in a collision with Brian Clough that had resulted in Cloughie suffering a serious cruciate-ligament injury.

There were other good players around at that time, too. George Jones was an up-and-coming striker, Alec Alston also played up front and there was Tommy Claxton. They were all good players and loyal club men.

My favourite games were against our great rivals Bolton Wanderers. One Friday night, there was a crowd of over 23,000 packed into Gigg Lane and my future City teammates Francis Lee and Wyn Davies were playing for Bolton. Franny scored their consolation goal from the penalty spot: a sign of things to come! It was a fantastic atmosphere, especially in front of a crowd that was much bigger than average, which was around

5,000 to 10,000 in those days. We beat Bolton 2–1 that night and it was one of my best experiences at Bury.

I remember another of my future City teammates, Tony Book, coming to play against us with Plymouth Argyle. They used a sweeper system, which was a strange tactic in those days. It worked for them, though, because we played them twice in the space of just a few weeks and they beat us both times. Booky played in the sweeper role, though, of course, it was their coach, Malcolm Allison, who was responsible for them playing those unusual tactics. He was always way ahead of his time.

I scored my first senior hat-trick in a 6–1 win against Swindon Town in August 1964. Yet another of my future teammates, Mike Summerbee, played for the opposition that day. I remember their goalkeeper being injured during the match and Mike being forced to play for part of the game at right-back.

I'd always been a quiet lad away from the football pitch, a bit of a loner, really, though I never lacked confidence and had no problems mixing with the other players. However, it did come as a bit of a shock when, at the age of 19, I was asked to captain Bury's first team.

I was the youngest skipper in the football league. Brian Turner, who was much older than me, had been the captain and had served the club loyally for many years, so it certainly felt daunting when it was taken off him and given to me.

There was no aggravation from the other lads, no problems at all. It was a culture shock, though, and I didn't know what was expected of me at first. I still felt like I was just one of the lads, although as the games went on I felt more and more confident in the role.

I was the type of person who believed in my ability and the best way to captain the side, in my opinion, was to lead by example. I'd try to encourage my teammates to make sure they were in position or marking the right person, that sort of thing. I just kept it simple to begin with.

I suppose after I'd been made captain at Bury, at such a young age, more people from outside the club would have started taking notice of me. Although I was becoming aware that scouts from the bigger clubs were visiting Gigg Lane, I never let it affect me. As far as I was concerned, I thought I would finish my career at Bury because I was so happy there, although I did have ambition to play at the highest level.

In my spare time, I used to go and watch the other teams in the area. I saw Stockport County on a few occasions, because they played on Friday nights. Whenever I could, I'd go and see City or United, though I ended up at Maine Road more often than Old Trafford.

I can't say I did that because of any feelings for either club, it was just more convenient to watch City. I used to enjoy watching Glyn Pardoe and Neil Young play in those days. I remember being at Old Trafford on a Wednesday night when Dave Mackay, playing for Spurs, broke his leg in a collision with Noel Cantwell.

About that time, I switched my lodgings, moving to stay with Mrs Girling at Whitefield on the Sunnybank Estate. Bury had made the suggestion to relocate because there were a couple of other players also in digs at Sunnybank, John Bain and Ernie Yard, the latter of whom emigrated to South Africa in later life.

John Bain and I became big friends. In fact, a few years later, he was best man at my wedding and I was best man at his. Another of my mates was John Rawlingson, a skinny centre-half who was the life and soul of the dressing-room. He was the sort of lad who used to laugh at his own jokes. It's no surprise that he went on to be a professional comedian after his playing days. He's known as 'Spike' and works regularly at St James's Park on a match day.

Spike maintains that although I was a modest lad I had a wicked sense of humour. He reminded me recently of a game we played for Bury at Southampton, when John Hollowbread, the former Spurs keeper, was in goal. Spike told me, 'I remember you scoring at The Dell in a game we lost but you still had the confidence to slot one away and tell Hollowbread to pick that one out and that you'd be back to score another one in a minute.

'My first impression of Colin was that he looked too skinny to be a footballer. He couldn't have been more than ten stone wringing wet. He was fast, though, and boy could he run. At first, he was difficult to get to know and he certainly didn't suffer fools gladly. He had a great sense of humour. He's dry and sarcastic and you have to be on your guard against him.

'I'd joined Bury just a short time before Colin and because we both came from the North-east there was a natural affinity between us. I grew up in Wallsend and we became good friends. He wouldn't speak his mind out loud very often but to people like me and John Bain, another of his close friends, he'd always speak his mind.

'Colin grew up in Hesleden, which is the sort of place that has tumbleweed blowing through it these days. It's not the same now that the coal mines have closed. I worked at a club in Hesleden recently. I did a one-night stand, though it felt more like a month's hard labour. They were a tough audience to get laughs from. I'd sum Colin up by saying he's got a wicked sense of humour and, of course, he was a great, great footballer.'

It's funny how other people see you, isn't it?

I can certainly remember that in those days it was a real battle just to get a new pair of football boots. The club gave us a small budget to sort ourselves out and we'd get the best we could from the local shop.

I was never really into girls at that time, all I was bothered about was training and playing, though John Bain used to take me along to the local dancehalls from time to time. We also used to play snooker regularly, above Burtons on the Rock, in Bury town centre. There were about eight tables in there with John Spencer, the future world snooker champion, who was from nearby Radcliffe, always on table number one. It's hard to believe these days that the world's number one would do his practising down at the local snooker hall, but he did!

They were great days and a perfect apprenticeship for what lay ahead. I was happy and had no desire to move on but more and more clubs were hoping to tempt me away from Bury. Harry Godwin was the chief scout at Manchester City at the time and he recommended me to their coach, Malcolm Allison, and manager, Joe Mercer. Blackpool were the other club who wanted to sign me. They were struggling in the First Division while City were doing well in the Second Division, looking a certainty for promotion.

I've talked to Malcolm many times about those key moments in my life. This is his version of events.

'Colin was pointed out to me by Paul Doherty, a journalist who I knew quite well at that time, and Harry Godwin had also sent back good reports. They told me there was a kid at Bury who was going to be very good. I valued Paul's opinions, as they were always accurate. As a result of that advice, I went to watch him play and he did quite well, though he was only a teenager at the time.

'I took a second look at him in a midweek game and then after a third visit I asked Bury how much they wanted for him. They told me they wanted £45,000, which was a lot in those days, more than we had available immediately.

'I told them they were asking too much for such a young player and left the negotiations. I carried on going to watch him, though, and would sit in the stands at Bury telling everyone within earshot that he was hopeless in the air and too one-footed, to try to put any other interested clubs off from trying to sign him. My patience paid off, because we eventually signed him for £45,000 a few weeks later.'

Perhaps it was for the best that Malcolm tried to prevent me moving elsewhere; who knows what might have happened had I gone to another club. It was quite strange how the move to City came about, from my perspective. It certainly came out of the blue and was completed very quickly.

Bert Head was now the manager at Bury. He told me about the interest in me from City and Blackpool while sitting in his car, which, for me, was a rarity in itself. I could hardly fit into the passenger seat because of all the discarded fish and chip papers.

Bert always used to watch the trial matches, up in the stand, eating his lunch. It was certainly an interesting smell with him in that car, stale fish and chips mixed with the sweat and muck associated with playing football.

Bert took me for transfer talks at both clubs. I think Bury were short of cash, so they wanted to do a deal before transfer deadline day. I chose Manchester City in the end because of the feeling of ambition that existed at the club. They were definitely the team on the up at that time.

I can't remember how much money Blackpool offered me, because it wasn't an important part of my decision and I had no idea what fee Bury would receive for the transfer. Although Malcolm Allison and Joe Mercer were to become the men who influenced my career the most, neither played a part in my decision. I didn't meet either of them during the period of negotiation.

I remember it being a busy day for transfer deadline moves.

On that spring day in 1966, as well as my move to City, Rodney Marsh went from Fulham to Queens Park Rangers for £15,000 and Allan Clarke moved from Walsall to Fulham for £35,000. Bury received £45,000 from City, beating the previous transfer record of £42,500 paid by Tottenham for teenager Cyril Knowles on his move to White Hart Lane.

My wages at Bury had been £25 a week. City lifted that figure to £35, which was wonderful, and they gave me a three-year contract, which was longer than average in those days. I never really had the opportunity to say goodbye to the Bury supporters when I moved to City because it happened so quickly and it was with some mixed feelings that I moved on. Naturally, I was excited about the prospect of playing in the First Division and it looked likely that City would win promotion.

The family, back home in Hesleden, never influenced my decision about leaving Bury and their attitude was that as long as I was happy, they were happy. My new improved wage wasn't enough to buy my own house, so I remained in digs with Mrs Girling in Whitefield. I could now afford a car, though. My first was a Ford Cortina, registration number SEN 113. I bought it second-hand from a garage on Manchester Road, Bury, and used to travel back to Hesleden in it.

It was a long journey home, especially since I'd have to go via Burnley, Nelson and Colne doing no more than 40 mph. There were no motorways in those days, so it would take up to five hours to complete the journey. I drove cautiously because I didn't want to be caught speeding so soon after passing my test!

I was more than happy living at Mrs Girling's. I used to push her husband, Percy, to the local pub, The Bluebell, in his wheelchair but never went in for a drink. I didn't think it was the right thing for a footballer to be seen doing, even if it was just a soft drink. My sister Eileen often stayed at The Bluebell when she came to visit me.

I loved my time at Bury and have many happy memories from those three years at Gigg Lane. Later in life, I played golf with Bob Stokoe, the manager who'd signed me for Bury. He was a better player than me, so he gave me a shot a hole, except on the par threes. We were playing for a brand-new golf ball. I won the game at the final hole.

I remember him mumbling under his breath as he got out the new ball he had in his pocket. He dropped it, very purposefully, on the green in front of me. 'There's your prize,' he said. 'You pick it up if you want it!' He couldn't bear to hand it to me. He remained a bad loser several years after retirement.

CHAPTER THREE
Arrival at City

My first day at Maine Road as a Manchester City player was really quite strange, because none of the first-team players were there. Malcolm Allison had taken them away to a training camp at Lilleshall, the Football Association's training base in the Midlands.

I walked in through the main entrance of the club. It was something I'd never done before as a spectator and I was immediately impressed with the size of the place compared to Bury. One of the first people I met was Mike Summerbee, who wasn't with the other City players because he was recovering from flu. I was immediately struck by his confidence and how well he got on with everybody.

He had an enviable personality in that he could chat to anybody, whatever type of person they were and whatever their background. He talked to me like we'd known each other for years. If that had been me, I would have been polite enough to say hello but couldn't have been as outgoing as he was. He went out of his way to show me around the ground, introducing me

48

to everyone from the groundsman, Stan Gibson, to the secretaries and tea ladies. I'm such a quiet person, so I admire people like Mike Summerbee. To be a confident orator like him must be brilliant.

I couldn't fail to be impressed by what I saw at City and I was eager to meet my new teammates and play my first game for the club. The following day, Mike, Joe Mercer and I travelled down to join the rest of the players at Lilleshall.

On arrival, the first thing that impressed me was the huge hall: totally different to the surroundings I'd been used to at Bury. Johnny Hart welcomed us and guided me upstairs to show me where I'd be sleeping. Johnny had been a player at City for 16 years before becoming a member of the coaching staff.

We were to sleep in a huge dormitory that looked like a hospital ward with beds that had individual rails with curtains hanging down. The first thing I noticed was that the bed I'd been assigned had no blankets, sheet or pillow on it. My blankets *were* there but knotted around the curtain rail. I spent half an hour untying them, wondering what sort of team I'd joined! It was a fantastic feeling, though, to be part of such a bubbly group.

That first night, they started pinging a golf ball around the room, over and under the beds. The ringleaders of the fun and frivolity, at that time, were Ralph Brand and Johnny Crossan. It was a great atmosphere, as of course it should have been, as City were looking certain of promotion with only 11 games to go.

My debut came at the Baseball Ground, against Derby County. I've never lacked self-confidence as a player, so I wasn't any more nervous than for any other game. I was always one of the quieter players in the dressing-room, even during my days as captain at Bury, so I was hardly likely to be much different making my debut for City. I'd spent so much time playing football on my own as a youngster that it had just become part of my nature to prepare in isolation.

There were one or two, like Summerbee and Mike Doyle, who'd say, 'Come on, let's get at 'em', or something like that, geeing everybody up. Alan Oakes and Glyn Pardoe were more like me, the types who'd quietly go through their own routine. I just mulled around, trying to get rid of the butterflies fluttering around in my stomach. I visited the toilet a few times and then it was time to go up the tunnel and get on with it.

The crowd was bigger than those I was used to with Bury, with just under 25,000 there that day to see us win 2–1. Just as I had done at Bury, I managed to score on my debut, which made it all the more enjoyable. It wasn't my best-ever goal, it just hit my backside and went in but they all count.

I sat in the stands watching the next couple of games against Everton in the FA Cup – I'd already played for Bury in the competition, so I was cup-tied. Once again, it was Mike Summerbee that made a big impression on me. He was definitely a bit of a joker. I was watching him carefully while the rest of the fans were following the ball. He and Everton's Sandy Brown seemed to spend most of the time elbowing each other in the teeth or smacking each other around the ear. That sort of thing didn't happen at Bury!

Sometimes it was Mike who started stuff like that but most of the time it was the other way around. People used to kick wingers early on in the game and the majority would lie down and die, and the defender would make the game easier for himself. If you kicked Summerbee, you riled him and it would be twice as bad for *you*. They don't come any braver and harder than Mike Summerbee. He's opinionated, too – here's his view of me!

'He was fantastically fit, a big step above us and we were a very fit side ourselves. On the field, he was a bit of a yapper, having a go at people, especially referees. He's a very shy person and maybe he could have worked a bit on that side of his personality. He stood out like a bottle of Dom Perignon champagne in a case of Tizer.'

I told you he was opinionated! I played up front in my first few games for City as one of the two main strikers. I thoroughly enjoyed it, basically working from the halfway line and into their box. When I look back on things now, there are times when I feel sorry that I didn't play up front more often. It saved my energy, working in the opposition half.

As time moved on, my role was to work *between* the two penalty areas. It was Malcolm's idea that I played in midfield. Perhaps I would have enjoyed the glory side of things if I'd stayed up front.

I didn't have to wait long to play against my old Bury teammates; in fact, we played them twice within a few days. First it was a 1–0 win at Maine Road on Good Friday with the trip to Gigg Lane coming the following Tuesday. They made me captain for my return to Bury. We made the same mistake that day as the City team I'd scored against on my debut for Bury. We underestimated them, expecting to win easily.

I was proud to skipper the side for the occasion and it was great to be back at Bury and say goodbye to all the friends I'd made there, although the day was spoiled by our 1–2 defeat. I was only City captain that one night – I hope the defeat wasn't the reason they took it off me!

We clinched our inevitable promotion at Rotherham on 4 May 1966. There had been no real pressure on us at Millmoor that day, with four more games remaining, but, nevertheless, we wanted to win. The changing-rooms were fairly basic and almost totally constructed from wood. You could shake hands with the person opposite you because it was so narrow, unlike the big square rooms in most grounds.

I don't remember much about the game, although I know that by half-time my ankle was very swollen. They couldn't take me off because there were no substitutions allowed, so they strapped my ankle on the outside of the boot. If I'd taken the boot off, I probably wouldn't have got it back on again. I played like that throughout the second half. It was during that period, playing down the hill, that I scored the vital goal to give us a 1–0 win and secure our place in the First Division. I don't think I've been back to Rotherham since.

That was the first day I tasted champagne. Malcolm had probably been carrying it around for the previous two games, ready for when promotion finally came. It seemed the perfect way to celebrate and there were to be many more opportunities to celebrate during my time as a player with Manchester City.

I was noticing that there was something truly special about City. I'd enjoyed my apprenticeship at Bury because it was so homely and although City was much bigger, it had a similar feel. We were all part of the same family. First-team players would pop into the laundry room and have a cup of tea with the ladies who worked in there. I quickly felt like part of the Maine Road furniture.

I was getting to know the City players quite well by now and found them to be very different personalities. The captain was Johnny Crossan, who was not only a great player but also the life and soul of the dressing-room.

Neil Young made a big impression on me, too. As a newcomer to the team, I was determined not to make a fool of myself in training, so I tried to keep everything simple. Youngy came running towards me, in a one-on-one, and he did something I could never do. I was looking him in the eye one moment and the next he wasn't there! I looked over my shoulder and he'd gone past me with no effort at all.

He seemed to be able to roll past you without really trying. I could beat someone with an instinctive movement but if I had time to think about it, I was useless. Youngy could go past you like you weren't there, on either side. If he'd been braver, he would have been one of the best players in the world. In terms of skill, beating people and scoring, he *was* great but he used to frustrate supporters because he never liked to challenge on the halfway line for those big kicks from the goalkeeper. He used to duck underneath it or do anything else he could to reduce the risk of inflicting pain on himself.

When I was with Bury, I'd read the *Football Pink* and you could guarantee that one of the City scorers each week would be Young. He had a great shot, although the key to it was not the power with which he hit the ball but the quality of the swing – a bit like a golfer. He kicked the ball with very little bend or swerve and they went as straight as an arrow. Despite his lack of bravery, you certainly didn't mind having Youngy in your side. He had quality written all over him.

I quickly developed close friendships with Glyn Pardoe, Mike Doyle and Alan Oakes. Doyley was desperate to win, like me. He used to have a bit of a temper and had to be pulled away from fights in the tunnel on at least a couple of occasions. I'm not sure what had made him that way, perhaps it was because he was a local lad and he'd grown up as a City supporter. Oakey and Glyn were quiet, like me, and the four of us socialised together on the long away trips.

Oakey might have shared the quieter nature of my personality but, just like me, he always gave 100 per cent. No one could ever question his commitment, though I do remember Malcolm once criticising him during the half-time break. He usually kept quiet but this time he rose to his feet, took off his shirt and threw it down in the middle of the dressing-room. It was soaked in sweat and plopped loudly as it landed on the floor.

The dressing-room went silent. You could have heard a pin drop, until after what seemed an age but was probably just a few seconds, he said, 'Here you are, see if you can do any better.' No one said anything. His commitment was never questioned again.

After beating Rotherham, we had two successive games in London, at Orient and Charlton. We travelled down for those games the day before, so we had the Friday night to ourselves. Oakey, Doyley, Glyn and I would go and watch a film together. Wherever one went, the other three went. It wasn't that we were being cliquish but you always pair off, or go in small groups, with people who have personalities like yours or with whom you feel comfortable. There was no friction between the different little groups we split into; it was just the way it worked out.

My first summer at City was spent watching England win the World Cup. It was an event that was to give everyone involved in football in this country a massive boost. Like most people, I watched what I could on the TV and dreamt of playing in the same team as Bobby Moore, Bobby Charlton, Martin Peters, Geoff Hurst and Gordon Banks. Once it had finished, my next goal was to continue to do my best for City in the First Division and hope that one day I might get the chance to play for England, too.

I spent most of that summer back in Hesleden. I played cricket, when I could, for the team at nearby Castle Eden. My relationship with Dad had become closer by then. He'd remarried but wasn't really happy with his life at that time. He showed his feelings more easily and we developed a very good understanding. He was certainly very proud of the way my career was going.

When I returned to City for pre-season training, there hadn't been many changes. Joe and Malcolm largely stuck with the team they'd built in Division Two, though they did sign the full-back, Tony Book. I remembered being impressed with him when he'd played as a sweeper for Plymouth against Bury. He was 32 years old, though he told us he was 30. I think he was a little embarrassed that he'd joined a First Division club so late in his career.

Malcolm had been Booky's coach at Plymouth and it didn't take the rest of us long to see why he rated him so highly. He was very quick and had plenty of skill. He made his debut at Southampton in a 1–1 draw and he soon became one of my best friends both on and off the pitch.

The build-up to my first derby game against Manchester United couldn't have been more exciting. There'd been a buzz around town for about a fortnight before the game and people had been asking for tickets for a month beforehand. Mike Doyle particularly enjoyed those games. He never hid his dislike of United and showed a commitment and passion for them like few others.

It was 17 September 1966 and City hadn't played at Old Trafford for four years. United had Best, Law and Charlton in their side. I'd watched Denis Law on a few occasions when I'd been at Bury. He was a lethal finisher, with his head or his feet, and I would say he scored eight or nine times out of every ten chances. Inevitably, he scored the winner that day.

It was a bad-tempered game which the referee, Jack Taylor, struggled to control at times. It proved to be a major disappointment but the man who felt it most was Malcolm. He was furious. He felt we'd believed the hype that United had created and that they'd psyched us out. He was determined we'd never live in their shadow again while he was the coach.

I was getting to know Joe Mercer and Malcolm Allison better by now. Joe was the manager and Malcolm his assistant. Joe did the office work and television interviews, and Malcolm ran the coaching side and anything to do with training. Malcolm's personality dictated the side. Their relationship was perfect, like father and son. I never saw any tension between them.

On the Friday before a game, Joe would say a few words, perhaps telling us a bit about the opposition. Malcolm would be more detailed, telling us how to take our corners and defend those from the opposition. The team talk was the same every week. They were like a double act and knew exactly what they were doing.

Malcolm used to vary training as much as possible so it didn't become boring. We never knew what to expect. For example, more than once we turned up at the ground and he'd arranged for a coach to take us to Blackpool. He'd take us to the swimming baths in the town, where we'd have a sauna, massage or brine bath.

We used to play five-a-side on the beach and one time the tide started to come in quicker than expected. A few of the lads pointed out to Malcolm that we were fast being surrounded by water but he told us to carry on playing. By the time we stopped, the water was five feet deep and we had to cross twenty-five yards of it to get back to shore.

Johnny Crossan couldn't swim and was petrified. He jumped onto Malcolm for a piggyback. Both of them were floundering at times as they struggled through the sandy water. Can you imagine the headlines if either of them had drowned?

We stopped at the Norbreck Hotel in Blackpool on a couple of those occasions. One evening I'd been out with a couple of the lads and we must have been making a bit of noise. Stan

Horne pushed his bedroom door ajar to tell us to quieten down. He was completely starkers!

I grabbed hold of him around the shoulders and pulled him into the lift. Someone else pressed the lift button and we were on our way to the ground floor. As the door slid open we were faced with two old women, me in my best suit, Stan in his birthday suit. I can still hear them screaming now!

CHAPTER FOUR
They Called Me Nijinsky

Malcolm Allison gave me the nickname Nijinsky – not after the Russian ballet dancer but the legendary racehorse. The sporting thoroughbred won the 2,000 Guineas, Epsom Derby and St Leger. The man who rode Nijinsky into the record books, Lester Piggott, described the horse as the greatest he ever rode. That's quite a nickname to live up to but it was nice to be compared to such a great winner, especially since I enjoy racing myself.

I had other nicknames, too. The supporters started calling me 'The King', which led to Glyn and Oakey calling me 'The Baron' and Doyley referring to me as 'His Eminence'. Those nicknames meant more to me than any other type of adulation.

All my teammates were great players, so to think they had that kind of respect for me was a wonderful feeling. Malcolm clearly thought a lot of me, too, because when I asked for an occasional extra day off, so I could go back to visit the family in Hesleden over the weekend, he never said no. The other lads used to tease me about that.

The only problem with being known as Nijinsky is that it

made some people think my game was just based on running and stamina. It's true that I did enjoy running, though. I've always been naturally fit and my resting pulse rate is in the low 40s. Joe Lancaster used to train us in Wythenshawe Park on Mondays – and, boy, did we train hard. It was about a five-mile course around the park and at regular intervals we'd stop and do various exercises. After the run, we'd go onto the track and do the serious stuff.

We'd split into two groups and each would sprint half the track before jogging across the middle while the others took their turn. We'd start by sprinting 200 metres, then 150, 100, 50 and 20 metres before going back up through the same intervals to 200 metres. It was hard work. Joe used to tell me that I could have been a successful middle-distance runner.

I used to do a running commentary for the City lads when we were doing the longer runs. They'd be blowing, at both ends, and could hardly breathe, and I'd come up on the outside saying, 'And Red Rum comes up to join the leaders and looks like he's coasting.' You can imagine the language I got back off them.

Malcolm says the athlete Derek Ibbotson had watched me at one training session and said I'd have been a world champion if I'd been an athlete rather than a footballer. I think in games I was just as tired as the rest but I had a quicker recovery rate and I never wanted to give less than my best.

During mid-November of my first full season with City, we played Everton at Maine Road. Alan Ball, who I'd watched during the summer helping England win the World Cup, was at the heart of their midfield. Everyone seemed keen to compare the two of us, though of course he was far better-known than me. I prepared for the match in my usual way and didn't let the comparisons affect my game. We won 1–0 and I scored the winner.

We were nearer the bottom of the table than the top, though, as we headed into the New Year. It took a 1–1 draw in my first Maine Road derby to finally get us believing in ourselves after a run of five games without a win and just one goal – mine against Southampton – to show for our efforts.

The 1966–67 season was one of consolidation. We finished 15th and I appeared in every league game, scoring 12 goals. We had a great run in the FA Cup and, although we lost to Leeds United in the quarter-finals, we were starting to be recognised as a team with much potential.

Leeds was one of the great sides of that era. Don Revie was their manager and among their players that day were Billy Bremner, Eddie Gray and Jack Charlton, who bundled in the only goal in controversial fashion. The media described the match as the best of the year and praised our adventurous approach.

Towards the end of that season, Malcolm had persuaded Joe Mercer to sign Tony Coleman, a player whose reputation for trouble was well known. Joe knew what Coleman was like, having been on a course at Lilleshall when 'TC' had thrown a bed through a window. However, Malcolm knew what he was doing and Joe trusted him.

We had a great pre-season, with Coleman and Johnny Crossan in fine comic form as we travelled to West Germany and Belgium, though Crossan was to join Middlesbrough before the start of the new season. He'd been involved in a car crash the previous year and had never quite reproduced his best form, so Malcolm thought it was time for him to move on. Doyley and Glyn had, by now, both been moved into defence, so Malcolm was on the lookout for attackers.

We started the season slowly, drawing with Liverpool before losing to Southampton and Stoke. Things had improved considerably by the time we played United at Maine Road in late September. Paul Hince had helped turn things around with a few dazzling wing performances and Ken Mulhearn was making his debut in goal, replacing Harry Dowd, who had a dislocated finger. We lost the game 1–2, though I did score our consolation goal. Two games later, at home to Wolves, we had the new striker Malcolm and Joe had been so desperately looking for. They'd remembered Francis Lee playing for Bolton Wanderers against City in the Second Division and from a League Cup tie played the previous year. For some reason, Franny had apparently threatened to walk out on Bolton and it suited him to move to another local club because he was already starting to build his business empire.

Franny's lifestyle was made up of two major ingredients: he'd come and do his training and then go and pursue his business interests. His number one priority was football but once we'd finished training he'd be the first changed and away. He was probably smarter than the rest of us, too. We hardly saw him after training he was so dedicated to his business.

Franny and I weren't really pals off the field and we had our own friends within the team. Later in our playing careers, whenever there were birthdays or anniversaries we'd go to each other's houses, perhaps for a Christmas party or other celebration, but we didn't socialise together at weekends. Franny was different to me, not that it mattered.

I'm not a judgemental person; I accept people as they are and he was fine. Franny's character was more like Mike Summerbee. Although they didn't seek out the limelight, it certainly didn't bother them if it came along. They'd just take things in their stride.

Franny's arrival in the team prompted a run of results that saw us climb up the table, winning six and drawing two of the next eight games. Next up were Tottenham at Maine Road, on a frozen pitch. The game would never have been played today. It became known as the 'ballet on ice' and, just like our FA Cup tie against Leeds the previous season, it was described by those who were there, or saw it on *Match of the Day*, as the game of the season.

Tottenham's side was full of internationals like Jimmy Greaves, Dave Mackay, Joe Kinnear and Pat Jennings. They took the lead through Greaves but with the help of extra grip from the sharpened studs we wore, we waltzed back to win the game 4–1, our goals coming from Summerbee, Coleman, Young and me.

By the season's halfway point, we were third in the table, just behind Manchester United and Liverpool, but successive defeats to West Brom soon brought us back down to earth. Encouraged by a 7–1 FA Cup thrashing of Reading at Elm Park, we went on a run of six league wins, ended by a draw against Arsenal. We'd climbed to the top of the table, before a defeat at Leeds.

The derby match at Old Trafford on 27 March 1968 was to prove a key moment in our season. Malcolm reminded us that United considered themselves top dogs and warned us not to be overawed by the hype surrounding them, as we had been the season before. Well, within a minute it looked like we would suffer another defeat, with George Best giving them an early lead and Booky blaming himself for the goal.

We dug in for a while before slowly taking control of the game. After 15 minutes, I managed to score the goal that drew us level. After half-time, we were dominant, taking the lead through George Heslop and completing the victory with a penalty from Franny Lee after I'd been brought down in the box. The only downside to that very special evening was that I suffered a knee injury that was to keep me sidelined for the next four games.

City hadn't won the League Championship, the biggest honour in English football, since the 1930s and it was gradually occurring to everyone that we could be on the verge of writing ourselves into the history books. As a boy, I'd dreamed of playing for England, winning the title and the FA Cup. A few more wins and I could be about to help my club become the best team in the country.

We lost both of our next games, dropping to third place. It looked as if our title hopes were slipping away but three successive wins against Sheffield Wednesday, Everton and Spurs meant that the Championship would be decided on the last day of the season. We had to win at Newcastle or hope United, who had a better goal average, slipped up against the team I'd supported as a boy, Sunderland.

I believed in horses for courses and Newcastle wasn't a ground I'd been to often and got a result. As a matter of fact, apart from the championship-deciding game, the only other result I remember getting there was a 0–0 draw, which I think was in the cup.

It wasn't a happy hunting ground as far as I was concerned. Winning at Spurs the week before had been less of a problem because their style of football suited us and more often than not we got the points against them. Going to Newcastle was different.

The build-up to that game was different, too. The players used to receive two complimentary tickets each, which was never going to be enough for me. I knew the championship was going to be decided that day and my family wasn't far away in Hesleden. It felt like I had to try and find tickets for two coachloads of relatives and I didn't know how I was going to manage it.

Naturally, my dad and sister, Eileen, came to the game,

although I wasn't going to let the fact that they were in the crowd affect my nerves; and, anyway, the bigger the game the more butterflies I had and the better I played.

We had to win at St James's Park. The script couldn't have been written better for me. Sunderland, my boyhood team, were expected to be turned over easily by United. We went in all square, 2–2, at half-time. Malcolm was trying to keep the score at Old Trafford from us; he kept fobbing us off when we asked him. In the end, we found out that they were drawing too, before we went out for the second half. There was 45 minutes of the season left and it was all in the balance.

We won the game 4–3 to claim the title, although we'd made it a nerve-jangling last ten minutes when they pulled a goal back after we'd been leading 4–2. We couldn't really have won the championship in a better way. The name of the game, as far as Malcolm was concerned, was to score more goals than the opposition. It had been end-to-end stuff. Just to make it even better, United had lost 1–2 at Old Trafford against Sunderland. The scenes at the end of the game at Newcastle were amazing, with everyone running onto the pitch.

Over the years, I must have spoken to 90,000 City fans who claim they were at Newcastle that day. In reality, there were 46,300 and most of them were well-behaved City fans. The odd one or two encroached onto the pitch each time we scored but it had been in single figures. The behaviour of the crowd was absolutely fantastic considering the importance of the match.

That day I couldn't tell who was supporting who. All I could hear was a terrific roar and to be honest I assumed it was *their* roar because we were away from home. There was no segregation of supporters and so it was only when we went back down the A1 that we realised the number of fans who'd been there to support us.

The traffic was virtually at a standstill as we tried to leave Newcastle and return to Manchester. It didn't matter, though; we were having a great time on the coach. Joe was orchestrating the celebrations, waving his arms around conducting us in a sing-song. Malcolm jumped off the coach at one stage and wandered in and out of the traffic, much to the delight of the City fans who were stuck in the jam with us.

Eventually, once we were moving, I couldn't believe the number of cars that passed the coach with scarves hanging out of their windows. It must have been in the thousands. About halfway back, we stopped at a restaurant on the A1, opposite Wetherby racecourse. As we went inside, Malcolm ordered the champagne. It flowed freely, as it had done two years earlier at Rotherham. Unusually for me, I ended up singing 'Blaydon Races' at the top of my voice to the rest of the lads as we continued our journey home.

It was a fantastic day. To think, after more than 40 games we'd finished top of one of the best leagues in the world. Once we got back to Manchester, most of us went for a night out and a few drinks to unwind. It was only for a couple of hours but we had a great time. Oakey and Glyn went straight home; they were never ones to go out on the town.

We didn't have a civic reception at that stage because we went on an end-of-season trip to America. Ironically, we were presented with the trophy three days later before a friendly against my old club, Bury, at Maine Road. We won the game 4–2, with Malcolm even making a brief appearance as a substitute late on, wearing a No. 8 shirt on his back. The crowd even shouted 'Allison for England'!

Our trip to Manchester Town Hall didn't take place until late July. There were about 500 people at the dinner-dance held in our honour and I remember that we (the players) left early. We were already in pre-season training and were on a total alcohol ban, so it hardly seemed appropriate to stay there for the entire evening.

As if winning the championship was not enough reward for our great season, 1968 was also the year I made my England debut. I'd played twice for the Under-23s already. One of the games was at Goodison Park and Glyn Pardoe and Mike Doyle played alongside me against Hungary. I'd nearly made my senior England debut against Spain but had to pull out with an injury – one that almost caused me to miss the title decider at Newcastle.

My debut came in May 1968, a 3–1 win against Sweden at Wembley. The goals that day were scored by Martin Peters, Roger Hunt and Bobby Charlton, which showed me, as if I needed reminding, how good the rest of the players were.

It is the proudest moment in every England player's career when you get that first call-up. I was still living in digs in Bury. The letter from the Football Association used to arrive at Maine Road. As I received many more of those letters during the years that followed, I came to know what was inside before I opened it but it always gave me a buzz. My chest blew out with pride. I never thought to save any of those letters. I threw them all away but often wish I'd kept just a couple as they were so special to me.

To be named in the England squad, alongside players who'd won the World Cup in 1966, was a tremendous honour. I'd had a couple of calls before that debut against Sweden, so I suppose you could say I was eased in. I didn't think of myself as competing against anyone in particular for a place. I could have played wing-half or my club position of inside-forward. I would have been happy to play anywhere.

My second appearance for England came in Hanover against West Germany as we prepared for the European Nations Cup finals in Italy that summer. I didn't actually play in Italy but I travelled as part of the squad and my abiding memory was of the problems I had with hay fever. I used to carry a handkerchief everywhere with me on the training ground. I'm sure there was a period of about four days when I never got out of bed, it was that bad.

I was sneezing and it felt like I had asthma. Even back home I used to have injections to try to keep it under control. They did all sorts of tests on me and discovered I was allergic to lots of different things, including dogs. These days, I don't seem to suffer anymore – it seems you grow out of it! There were times back then when it was frightening. I used to wake up in the middle of the night struggling to breathe.

To mix with the likes of Geoff Hurst and Martin Peters, who scored the goals in the 1966 World Cup final, as well as Bobby Moore, Bobby Charlton and the world's best goalkeeper, Gordon Banks, was unbelievable.

When the letter came from the FA about ten days before a game, it would also list the other players who'd been called up. Seeing my own name there, a miner's son, made me remember the dreams I'd had as a child while kicking the ball around in the backyard of Hesleden. It was actually happening to me! I was playing with the best players in the world. Life couldn't be better.

CHAPTER FIVE
The Price of Fame

I've never been an extrovert, so I struggled to deal with being recognised by the public, which by now was becoming commonplace. I'd often walk down the street in Manchester and kids would shout to me from the other side and point at me saying things like, 'You're Colin Bell, aren't you?' I'd shout back, 'No. You've mistaken me for someone else, I'm not Colin Bell.' I was worried that if I admitted it, lots of other people would start talking about me and pointing at me and I would feel even more uncomfortable.

I only wanted to be recognised when I was on the pitch. I've never wanted to be a celebrity. Nowadays the media glorifies positions of celebrity and members of the public seem to relish the idea of being famous. I'm a quiet person and I enjoy my own company. I was not, and am still not, a great orator, I preferred to let others do the talking; I just wanted to play football.

I still enjoyed cricket too, and during my summer trips home I continued to play for Castle Eden. Eileen's husband, Bart, was involved with the team and knew I enjoyed playing, having spent many hours throwing the ball at me in their backyard. Bart showed me the correct way to hold a bat, with the double 'V' down the handle.

I'm sure Bart would have preferred me to be a cricketer and I must admit I really enjoyed playing. The great thing about playing for Castle Eden was that the rest of the lads thought of me as one of them and not some big superstar. They didn't treat me any differently to anyone else and didn't shy away from me. I was just one of the boys, as if I'd lived in the village all my life.

The summers back home were refreshing but by July I was looking forward to playing football again. One of the rewards for winning the Football League Championship was a place in the European Champion Clubs' Cup (now known as the Champions League). It was the first time City had played in European competition and Malcolm Allison had bragged, in typical fashion, that we would, 'terrify Europe to death'.

The 1968–69 season started well enough. We beat the FA Cup winners, West Bromwich Albion, 6–1 in the Charity Shield, the traditional curtain-raiser, which was played on the home ground of the champions. Tony Book had been injured on our close-season tour to North America but we seemed to handle his absence well in that opening game and expected to carry on where we'd left off when the new season kicked off in earnest.

With new forward Bobby Owen (signed from Bury during the summer) in our line-up, we opened up with a 1–2 defeat at Liverpool. Although we beat Wolves 3–2 in the second game of the season, at Maine Road, it proved to be a slow start. After drawing 0–0 against United, we failed to win any of our next six league games.

Every game felt like a cup-tie. The team talk from the opposing manager undoubtedly included a reminder that we were the best team in the country and it felt like every other team had suddenly found another 10 per cent effort from somewhere. There were so many other good sides anyway, that it made it very difficult for us. By the time we had worked out what was happening, a dozen games had passed, which made it a hard season from start to finish.

When we faced the Turkish side, Fenerbahçe, in the first leg of the European Cup tie in Manchester on 18 September, we weren't in the best of form. We still expected to win, though. We had no experience against foreign teams and no English team had played a Turkish side in competition before.

They kicked lumps out of us and we ended up drawing 0–0. Two weeks later, we travelled to Turkey for the second leg with no idea of what was waiting for us. Our hotel was on a hill overlooking the stadium, which was situated below us in a valley. When we woke up at nine o'clock in the morning and opened the curtains, their fans were already queuing at the turnstiles and it was an evening kick-off.

The hostility in the crowd later that day, spitting and taunting us, was unbelievable. There were police with guns guarding the tunnel from where we emerged, as fans snarled down at us from above. There were fires in the stands. It was a frightening experience.

The way they'd played in the first leg at Maine Road seemed angelic compared to their dirty tricks at their own ground. They showed no respect and kicked us off the park. We didn't know how to handle it and lost the game 1–2. Our European dream was over, for that season at least.

We were already too far behind to win the league title again. All the teams in the First Division were good at that time. In those days, you could look at the opposition team listed on the back of the programme and pick out two or three good, creative players, or a couple of great defenders.

For example, Southampton bought a player from Burnley called Brian O'Neill. I think they just bought him to kick people and add a bit more steel to the side. They also had John McGrath at centre-half and Dennis Hollywood at left-back. They were tough, uncompromising players.

I wondered how we left their place alive sometimes; indeed, we lost there 0–3 that season. They had some wonderful players up front, too, like Sydenham, Paine, Channon and Ron Davies, so they could pass and play as well. That was typical of all the clubs.

I always found it a challenge to pit my wits against the 'name' players who had the biggest reputations. I enjoyed playing against Bobby Moore. You certainly didn't need eyes in the back of your head playing against Bobby, as you did against some of the less-cultured defenders around at that time. Bobby was always fair and clean in the tackle.

I also enjoyed being up against Norman Hunter, who was a completely different type of defender. He'd try and rattle you with a couple of strong challenges early on. He was hard but honest and could play. Apart from my City teammates, there was no one I'd rather have had in my team in the big games than Norman Hunter.

One of my tactics was to try and run my opponents into the ground, moving them around to tire them out, especially if they were man-to-man marking. I tried to put a bit of thought into it. I don't think there was ever a player who got the better of me for 90 minutes. Even if I wasn't getting the ball, I would keep making runs to create holes for my teammates to exploit, dragging the opposition players out of position.

The further the season progressed, the more I realised that there was a fine line between being champions and being in a relegation battle. Lady luck seemed to play a big part in whether we finished near the top or the bottom. We didn't play badly that season; the others just seemed to raise their game more than they had before we'd won the league.

The great highlight of the 1968–69 season was the FA Cup and I certainly think that luck played its part in that competition. Our journey to Wembley started with a 1–0 home win against Luton. I missed the two games against Newcastle in the fourth round because of a knee injury I'd got against Chelsea. One of our best players up at St James's Park had been young Tommy Booth, just 19 years old and breaking into the team at that time. The fifth-round draw took us to Blackburn Rovers, where we won 4–1 thanks to two goals each from Franny Lee and Tony Coleman.

We beat Tottenham 1–0 at Maine Road in the quarter-finals, which took us into the last four and a game against Everton. As if facing Jimmy Greaves and Alan Gilzean of Spurs hadn't been tough enough in the previous round, we knew Everton had a crack team, with Howard Kendall, Alan Ball and Colin Harvey in midfield and a good defence behind them.

They were like us: they could play and believed in their own ability from 1 to 11. Brian Labone was the England centre-half, Gordon West was in goal and they had big Joe Royle up front. To turn them over would be a good result. We felt our name was on the cup when Tommy Booth scored the last-minute winner that sent us through to the final.

Back in the 1960s, the FA Cup final was the highlight of the year for many people. Families used to gather around the television to watch the game, even if their team wasn't involved. Many of the villagers back in Hesleden, including my dad, watched me that way. My sister Eileen and brother-in-law Bart travelled down to Wembley.

Although I wasn't aware of it, Eileen says there was some

jealousy aimed at the family during this period. 'They used to think that Bart and I were trying to act above ourselves. Colin's success didn't make any difference to us, though of course we were very proud of his achievements. Most of the villagers understood and were fully supportive but there was some jealousy. We didn't want any reflected glory and we didn't let it bother us.'

I was determined that the success I'd had at City was not going to change me. I'm a reluctant hero, just an ordinary bloke. I know that people look on Bobby Charlton, who's also from the North-east, as a hero but he's an ambassador all over the world, so that's understandable. I suppose in Chester-le-Street, Bryan Robson would have been idolised. I'd simply like to think that, in my home village, they were proud of me playing in the FA Cup final.

We always tended to go away for a couple of days before the big games and we prepared at a place in Tring before the final. On the day of the match, there were thousands of fans on Wembley Way as we made our way towards the stadium in the team bus. They were well behaved and out for a special day and it was great seeing the twin towers as we neared the end of our journey. It was probably the only ground where they opened up the gates and you could drive the coach up the tunnel.

Wembley is the home of football and the place where you want to play above all others. I had the same feeling of exhilaration every time I walked up the players' tunnel, which was at one end of the ground behind the goal. I suppose because we were league champions we were expected to beat Leicester, who'd already been relegated, but we didn't feel any extra pressure. We just wanted to win, like we always did. The fact that there would be 100,000 people there to watch the game just made it even more special.

Before the game, we went out to walk on the pitch and soak up the atmosphere. Although I never enjoyed being interviewed, I remember talking to the BBC commentator Kenneth Wolstenholme behind one of the goals. Ken also interviewed Mike Summerbee and Francis Lee, who were far better at that sort of thing than I was.

The Wembley pitch wasn't as good as it had been when I'd played there on my England debut a year earlier. The surface was rutted and heavy, and I knew it would be difficult to play good-quality football that day.

Leicester had some good players in their side. A young Peter Shilton was in goal, their captain David Nish in defence and Allan Clarke up front. Clarke was voted man of the match but Neil Young's goal proved decisive and we added the FA Cup to the League Championship from the previous season. We knew we'd worked hard to win that day and applauded the Leicester team as they received their runners-up medals.

Although I've said that fame was not something I wanted, it's certainly true to say that I've always fully appreciated the way the City fans have been right behind me. It was about the time of the FA Cup final that I started noticing the song that is still occasionally sung today.

A pop group called Scaffold had a number one hit with 'Lily the Pink' late in 1968 and the City fans put their own words to it. 'We'll drink a drink a drink to Colin the King the King the King, he's the leader of Man City. He's the greatest inside-forward the world has ever seen!' You can imagine how proud it made me feel.

Football is a team game, though, and as much as I was happy knowing that the supporters thought I was doing OK, it should be made clear that we were all in it together. These days, people seem to think that our successful period was all down to Francis Lee, Mike Summerbee and me. That's simply not true.

Inevitably, the players that catch the eye are the goal scorers and makers. People never seem to talk about the great tacklers or readers of the game. Those who help protect the goalkeeper and the ones who stop the goals don't often feature in the headlines.

It's a team game and Francis, Mike and I appreciated that. We were no better than the rest of them. We were like a big family and without the others we would have been nothing. It was the press that always bracketed the three of us together. At club level and in the dressing-room, we were no different to anyone else. None of the three of us ever bragged that we'd won the game. We knew it was a team game and we had the right mix of different types of players.

Malcolm summed it up best when he said, 'The success we had was down to the team. Within the team, we had three really good players. Summerbee was a great athlete and very strong, Francis was a good goal scorer and Colin was a great all-round player. They were all good players.'

The fact that Francis, Mike and I scored many of the goals and grabbed the headlines meant that we were seen as the icing on the cake but we never set out to make it that way. I've never thought it was fair that City's golden times are remembered by some as the Bell, Lee, Summerbee era. The BBC made a video, years later, called *Soccer Legends: Lee, Bell, Summerbee*, and I never felt comfortable being part of it, but that's the way the media had always described it.

The three of us rarely socialised together. Mike and Franny would go out with their girlfriends but I never really joined them. We had different personalities. I certainly considered Mike as a friend, no doubt about that. As a player there was nobody better to have in your side and he always performed just as well in home and away games.

Most teams played with wingers and since I was an inside-forward he was the nearest person to me for most of the game. If I ever needed help, even when he was in a bad position, he'd always be there. You can't ask for any more. You could almost say he was my minder or protector. As far as I'm concerned, he took a lot of the weight, and what you might call 'the heavy mob', off my shoulders.

The fact that he had a more outgoing personality than me also helped. He was a different type of player and brought different assets to the side. You don't want 11 tacklers or 11 who are specialist headers of the ball; you need a team that are a mix of different qualities and that's what we had.

There's no doubt that Mike and Franny had an extra dimension to their personalities. They always took part in the annual Junior Blues pantomime; in fact, I don't think they even had to be asked. There weren't many of the players who wanted to be on stage but they would lend their hand to anything, acting the fool without any bother.

The Bell, Lee, Summerbee triumvirate was created by the fans and the media but I played with a lot of exceptional players, many of whom were at City long before I joined that side. Roy Cheetham helped me a great deal during my early days at the club and Harry Dowd had a great sense of humour. If you then include Neil Young, Mike Doyle, Glyn Pardoe, Alan Oakes and the others, you can see it was an impressive group of players. We could not have been the players we were, though, without Malcolm Allison.

CHAPTER SIX
Malcolm Allison

In my opinion, Malcolm Allison is the best coach that has ever been. Malcolm was the driving force behind the success we had at City. Guided by Joe Mercer, the combination of their characters was perfection personified. Joe steered all of Malcolm's energies and powers in the right direction. I believe Malcolm should have received more recognition for his abilities. These days, awards are handed out much more frequently and I believe something should be presented to him in view of his many achievements. He's put so much into football and there are still many people today who appreciate his contribution to the game.

Malcolm was a player at West Ham United before going on to be a coach at City and various other clubs, and he's dedicated his life to football. His flamboyance and pushiness is probably the reason he never received an OBE or MBE. There are similarities between Malcolm and Brian Clough in that respect. Cloughie received an honour later in his life, so why not Malcolm?

There were two sides to Malcolm: the flamboyant side, for the press, and the other side – that of a top coach and motivator. If you knew him personally, you knew he was a brilliant man. If you viewed him from afar, you could only judge him on what you saw in the press, with the cigars, the hats and the women on his arm, which I believe was all to sell newspapers. He loved both lifestyles. He loved working with players, being down to earth and getting the best from them, showing them how the game worked and motivating them. He loved football and he loved life.

As far as I'm concerned, his number-one skill was motivation. There is nobody better in life than somebody who appreciates what you do and gives you a pat on the back from time to time, and Malcolm did that often. I used to feel like I was on cloud nine when Malcolm put his arm around me; I'd feel I could give another 10 per cent.

I don't think Malcolm and I ever fell out or had any arguments. We came to know each other very well and there were never any problems. I'm not saying he never criticised me, but he knew my temperament and how to get the best from me.

Malcolm wanted us to win with style, the way the game should be played. His philosophy was that our basic aim was to score more than the opposition. That was the theme of my career at City; we didn't know any other way to play. If Malcolm had asked us to play differently, more negative and less entertaining football, we wouldn't have enjoyed it as much. I suppose we would have done whatever he asked but I certainly wouldn't have derived as much pleasure from it. Kicking people and grinding out results would not have suited me.

To me, playing football is not complicated. It's all about keeping the ball on the floor and stringing a few passes together, going from end to end and scoring a few goals. Tackles are also important and there's nothing wrong with a good hard challenge, but when you can, you've got to get it down and play – and that's what we did during Malcolm's time.

He was never short of ideas. He was one of the pioneers of making sure footballers eat the right kinds of food. I remember him importing a drink from America, which I think was glucose-based. It doesn't seem particularly radical now but it was at the time.

Another of Malcolm's great ideas was to bring in outsiders to introduce a fresh approach to training. He brought in Lennie Hepple, who was related to 'Pop' Robson, the former Newcastle and West Ham striker. Lennie worked with us on suppleness and dance moves. Outsiders may have thought it was a crazy idea but I thought it was great and it certainly helped my game.

Malcolm also introduced a sprinting routine that was based on techniques employed by the Olympic athlete Valeri Borzov. We started on the top of a little hill, about five yards above ground level, before gathering speed on descent and then sprinting flat out on the level surface.

Malcolm was always reading books and had us trying all sorts of different ideas. He'd read about the great American athlete, Jim Ryan, who ran a mile in under four minutes as a seventeen-year-old. His coach had been a guy called Bob Timmons, who had trained his protégé by making him run half a mile up to 105 times a week. All his sessions involved keeping in constant motion on the track during interval training, which became a technique Malcolm used with us to good effect.

On one occasion, he took us to Salford University and told us to wear gas masks. They were old rubber ones, the type that were handed out during the Second World War. As we struggled to get them on, I was desperately trying to work out how this was going to help me strike the ball better or improve my tackling! Once the mask was in place, it felt like it was stuck to my face and even before we started doing anything, I didn't seem to be able to inhale enough air. Malcolm revealed that the reason for this experience was to teach us the importance of breathing more efficiently.

Malcolm became friendly with a professor at the university and invited him to monitor me during a game. He was instructed to watch me carefully and he concluded that I ran between seven and nine miles and that I never walked, unless the game was dead. The professor even worked out how many times I'd been at half-pace and how many times I'd sprinted. After the game, he showed me the results displayed graphically.

Another time, he had me running around Wythenshawe Park with a box on my back that measured my heart rate and other physiological parameters. The exercise also involved evaluating recovery rates and it was fascinating.

As well as his unusual training methods, Malcolm used to think about psychology both from our perspective and that of the opposition. One of his favourite tricks was to get Stan Gibson, the groundsman, to flood the Maine Road pitch. He believed that if it was wet, more mistakes would be made and that would favour the team who scored more goals, which was generally us.

Malcolm and Stan didn't always see eye to eye on that subject because Stan always treated the pitch like the front lawn he never had. He used to stand at the end of the players' tunnel watching every divot that came out. It was his personal pride and joy.

There was a rumour in the newspapers around this period that Malcolm might be joining Coventry City as manager. We hadn't heard a denial and it was unthinkable to us that City would allow him to move away from Maine Road. I think we must have been playing at home that particular weekend. Things seemed to be coming to a head, so Mike Summerbee made a pre-emptive strike at the Friday team talk. He rose to his feet just as Joe Mercer started to stand. Mike asked Joe to sit down and give him two minutes to say a few things.

It was Mike who gave us the team talk that weekend, saying that if Malcolm moved on there would be 12 transfer requests on Joe's desk on Monday morning. Joe got back to his feet and said, 'They don't come much easier than that, these team talks! See you tomorrow.' Nothing came of the rumours. Whether there had ever been any truth in them, or whether Mike's speech had made any difference, we'll never know.

As a result of winning the FA Cup the previous season, we began the 1969–70 campaign at Elland Road facing the League Champions, Leeds United, in the Charity Shield. We lost the game 1–2 but started the new league season with an encouraging 4–1 win against Sheffield Wednesday at Maine Road.

Once again, as FA Cup holders, all the opposing teams seemed to be fired up that little bit more when they played us and we couldn't put together a run of consistent results, losing the next three games.

By mid-September, we'd won just three of our opening nine league matches, although we'd won 3–0 at Southport in the opening round of the League Cup.

By winning the FA Cup, we were back in European competition, this time in the Cup-Winners' Cup. I always enjoyed the challenge in Europe, playing against different styles of football. The games against Athletico Bilbao gave all of us the opportunity to make up for the disappointment of going out of the European Cup in the first round the previous season.

Our approach to European games wasn't really any different

to the way we played in the league. We tried to score as many goals as possible. We put six goals past Bilbao during the two games, though at one stage during the first leg in Spain we were 0–2 down. Having earned a hard-fought 3–3 away draw we won the second leg 3–0 to go through 6–3 on aggregate. In the next round, we put eight past the Belgian club, SK Lierse.

I always believed we could win every time we played at City. In fact, I always expected to be on the winning side in training, too, so when we were invited to play in the *Daily Express* five-a-side tournament at Wembley Arena on 6 November 1969, we went there to win.

Eight of us made the trip, including Oakey, Doyley, Glyn, and Neil Young with Dave Ewing as our coach. After our first couple of games, Dave came into the dressing-room with a fist full of fivers. 'Here you are, lads, here's your payment for that victory,' he proclaimed and handed us all a share. None of us realised we'd be rewarded financially for progressing further, so suddenly there was even more of a spring in our step; we couldn't wait for the next game.

We won the competition by beating Spurs 2–1 in the final, receiving several more cash payments along the way. We shared the money we made from winning that first national five-a-side tournament with the rest of the City players when we returned to Manchester the following day. It was the right thing to do – we were a team and that was the secret of our success.

Back in the First Division, we reached the middle of November in a decent run of form, having won three out of four in the league before facing United at Maine Road in the first of five derbies that season. We won that first game comfortably, 4–0, and I scored two of the goals.

The second derby of the season happened in the League Cup semi-finals, with the first leg at Maine Road on 3 December. We won that one 2–1. After taking the lead in the opening minutes, when I scored after Francis Lee's shot had taken a deflection, we thought we would hammer them again but Alex Stepney had a great game and we had to settle for just a one-goal advantage to take to Old Trafford.

I missed the second leg through injury. I was a bad spectator and became easily frustrated watching games in which I couldn't play, so I waited at home for news of the final score and whether we'd made it to Wembley again. Ironically, it was a mistake by Alex Stepney that booked our place in the final. With the score tied 3–3 on aggregate, 2–1 to United on the night, Francis Lee prepared to take an indirect free-kick on the edge of their penalty area.

I don't know whether Alex hadn't realised it was indirect or simply reacted out of instinct, but with Franny's shot going straight at goal Stepney instinctively blocked it, but Summerbee was onto it in a flash and turned the rebound into the net. That bit of quick thinking by Franny and Mike proved to be the winning goal and we were through to another cup final.

Although we were one win away from another trophy, we wanted to make sure we continued our progress in the Cup-Winners' Cup. After a long gap because of the winter break throughout Europe, we returned to action in early March against Academica de Coimbra of Portugal. It proved to be much more of a challenge than our other European games that season.

We drew the first leg 0–0 in Portugal, just three days before the League Cup final at Wembley. The journey home took much longer than expected because of bad weather, which meant we had to return via Birmingham rather than London. It was hardly the best preparation for such a big game. Just to make matters worse, the condition of the Wembley pitch was terrible. Snow had been swept off the surface and straw was laid on top to protect the pitch from any overnight frost.

The first five yards in from each touchline was like a swamp. The Horse of the Year show had been staged on the playing surface just days earlier, which had made things even worse. Sprinting down the touchlines was like running through treacle, while I could run twice as fast on the firmer ground.

What we didn't want to do, given the poor build-up to the game, was concede an early goal but Jeff Astle headed West Bromwich Albion into the lead with just five minutes gone. It took us an hour to get the equaliser through Mike Doyle but we couldn't avoid the one thing that none of us wanted: extra time.

This was where all those runs around Wythenshawe Park really paid off, because we were the stronger side in the extra 30 minutes, during which Glyn Pardoe got us the goal that won the cup.

Eleven days later, we beat Coimbra 1–0 in the return leg of the Cup-Winners' Cup quarter-final to earn a semi-final tie against Schalke 04 from West Germany. We lost the first game 0–1 in Gelsenkirchen, despite a wonderful performance from Joe Corrigan in goal during his debut season. The game was played in a stadium that looked like Altrincham's Moss Lane ground.

There was a seated stand on one side but the rest was just banking and terracing. At the time, I thought the crowd was about 15,000 to 20,000 but I've since found out there were probably far more packed into their tiny ground.

They were a good side, too, despite qualifying for the competition as runners-up in their domestic cup final to Bayern Munich. Their side included two German internationals, Reinhard Libuda and Klaus Fichtel.

It was a tough game in Germany and we were happy to return with a 0–1 defeat, knowing that we would fancy our chances of overturning the deficit at Maine Road. Our league form had been nothing special in the lead-up to the game. Having won 2–1 at Old Trafford, before the first leg in Germany, we failed to score in the three league matches that preceded the return game.

The semi-final second leg was one of our finest performances in Europe with Neil Young scoring twice plus one each from Franny, Mike Doyle and me. We won the game 5–1, earning a trip to Vienna for the final against Gornik Zabrze of Poland.

I always enjoyed the trips to Europe, because it was an excuse to have some fun as well as facing the challenge of a different type of opposition. We flew to Austria a couple of days before the game, allowing for some acclimatisation and a bit of sightseeing.

Our goalkeeper, Harry Dowd, was the type who always had his cine camera with him, a forerunner of today's video camera. The big difference between his old contraption and its modern equivalent was that there was no way of reviewing what you'd filmed until you had the film developed back home.

Harry had filmed everything in sight, the opera house, royal palaces . . . everything. He even brought his camera to team talks, which proved to be a big mistake. As we all sat waiting for Malcolm to come and have a chat to us, Harry left the camera on the table where three or four of us were sitting and nipped off to the toilet.

I think it was Mike Doyle who picked up the camera while Oakey dropped his shorts, showing off his manhood to the camera. By the time Harry returned, the camera was back in its place and we were sitting like innocent choirboys waiting to hear Malcolm's words of wisdom. The film was now X-rated stuff but Harry knew nothing about it.

When he returned to England, he invited his in-laws around for the first showing of the film. He hadn't checked it but got out his projector (a bit like Oakey!), rolled down the screen, closed the curtains and prepared for the première. No doubt he'd have been pointing out all the sights of Vienna as they watched the film together and then a sight of a different type would suddenly have appeared. I can only imagine the look of shock on his in-laws' faces!

The European Cup-Winners' Cup final took place on 29 April 1970. It was a wet miserable evening and the stadium hardly had any shelter for the supporters who'd made the trip from Manchester. It was a very strange game to play in. If we'd played the match in England or Poland, it would have been a full house. To stage it midway between the two, in the Prater Stadium in Vienna, where there was no local interest, made no sense to me. There wasn't much atmosphere because it was such a small crowd and the weather was so miserable.

I don't think there was ever any doubt that the game would go ahead. In those days, the majority of pitches were passed fit. The truth is that it was waterlogged and still would have been two days later, there was that much rain. There were pools of water all over the place. Once we got going, the ball stuck in the mud and you would have to go back and hook it out. It was a real farce. The game should never have been played, as the pitch was like a swimming pool.

It's a wonder that only Mike Doyle suffered an injury in the game, coming off with a bad ankle injury. We battled on through the mud, as we'd done twice at Wembley, to win the game, and the Cup-Winners' Cup, 2–1, thanks to a goal from Neil Young and a typical penalty from Franny.

The trophy was presented to us on the pitch, with the City fans huddled under the upper tier trying to keep dry. I couldn't see them very well because it was so dark and gloomy. In one way, it wasn't the best of nights, but we'd terrorised Europe, as Malcolm had threatened more than a year earlier; better late than never.

CHAPTER SEVEN
The Summer of 1970

By the spring of 1970, I was still living in digs and my life continued to be dominated by training and playing football, along with trips back to Hesleden to see my sister and dad. Most Saturday nights, after a game, I'd go into Manchester for a few drinks with friends from the Bury area. My favourite destination was the Portland Lodge, owned by the Williams brothers, who were big City fans.

I liked it there because no one bothered me. I used to have the odd Bacardi and Coke to unwind. I didn't have a skinful, just enough to take the nerves away.

One night, Tony Book introduced me to a beautiful blonde lady called Marie. It sounds a bit corny but our eyes met across a crowded room and from my point of view it was love at first sight. Booky tried to act as cupid. He knew Marie because his wife, Sylvia, was a regular in the Ashton-on-Mersey hairdressing salon that Marie owned.

Booky used to meet Sylvia at the salon and kept telling Marie to desert her usual social haunt, Blinkers, on the other side of town, and go down to the Portland Lodge, where he'd introduce her to someone special. Marie's friend, Yvonne Howell, whose brother was the City player Graham Howell, also played a part in bringing us together.

I've no idea why she was attracted to *me*. Marie had no interest in football and had never been to a match. As I chatted to her, I realised that the fact I was a footballer was irrelevant to her, which suited me fine. I took her phone number and promised to ring her when I returned from my trip to Mexico during the summer. I don't think she even watched the England games on TV but I knew that I wanted to see her again.

Winning four trophies in three seasons was the stuff I'd dreamed of as a boy in Hesleden and we'd won those honours playing entertaining football; life could not have been better. Being selected for the England squad that would defend the World Cup in Mexico was fantastic.

One of the benefits of that call-up was that I was given a Ford Cortina inscribed with the World Cup logo. Francis Lee and I went down to FA headquarters by train to appeal against one of his bookings for City. When we returned to the street in Manchester where I'd left my new car, it had gone.

After wandering the neighbouring streets, thinking I'd simply forgotten where it was parked, I realised it had been stolen. The car was found a few days later jacked up on bricks. The most upsetting aspect of the incident was that my favourite topcoat had been taken from the back seat. Still, I was going to the World Cup with England, so I wasn't going to let it bother me.

I'd been with the England squad to South America the summer before. We'd been to experience the weather conditions and sample the culture. The manager, Sir Alf Ramsey, thought it would be good preparation. We played in a couple of different countries and the tour lasted approximately three weeks.

We started the tour in Bogotá, Colombia, which is higher than Mexico, so it was the ideal way of becoming accustomed to playing at altitude. Adjusting to those conditions wasn't easy; it felt like you had asthma and reminded me of the feeling of wearing the gas mask at Salford University.

We returned to South America in the summer of 1970 as the favourites to win the Jules Rîmet trophy and many people believed our team was better than the one that had won it four years earlier. Alf gave us tablets containing salt and other minerals. He was well informed about what was needed, including the food, hotels and everything else we required.

As part of our build-up to the competition, we played a couple of friendlies. Our opening match was against Colombia, in Bogotá, on 18 May. The day proved to be a nightmare for our captain, Bobby Moore, who was arrested by the local police. He was accused of stealing a bracelet from the hotel gift shop. The story made the front pages of newspapers all over the world and threatened to disrupt our hopes of success.

We were told, after the incident, that the hotel we stayed in, the Tequendama, was well known as a place to con celebrities. The Green Fire jewellery shop was in the foyer and their trick was to say that something had been stolen so they could blackmail the person into paying some money before they were allowed to move on.

I heard that the great Brazilian player, Pelé, had been there a few months earlier and he had also fallen victim to the con but his club or the Brazilian authorities had paid up, so nothing ever appeared in the newspapers.

Our problems started when Bobby Moore and Bobby Charlton were in the shop together, looking for presents for their wives. The supposed incident happened as they tried to leave. They were told that an emerald and diamond bracelet was missing. It was Bobby Charlton they were after but Bobby Moore stepped in to take responsibility when he saw what was going on, because he felt he'd be able to deal with it better as he had a stronger personality.

After discussions with the police, we left the hotel and both Bobbys were allowed to travel with us for the game against Colombia. We beat them 4–0, with Bobby Charlton scoring one of the goals.

Our other warm-up match was in Ecuador but we had to fly back through Bogotá on our way to Mexico. When we landed, armed police arrested Bobby Moore and took him into custody.

We left for Mexico without him, which didn't seem right but we had no other option. He rejoined us two or three days later and he certainly looked rough when we saw him, probably through worry and lack of sleep.

He'd been kept in custody for so long because the Football Association refused to pay any money. As far as they were concerned, and of course they were right, no one was guilty of an offence. Eventually, it was cleared up but, of course, if the FA had paid up immediately, Bobby Moore would have been allowed to leave with us that day.

He rejoined us on 29 May, having taken part in a reconstruction of the supposed incident, which had proved he couldn't have committed the offence. His accuser, shop assistant Clara Padilla, had insisted he'd put the stolen necklace in his tracksuit pocket. Bobby's tracksuit didn't have any pockets and the item was never found!

Naturally, we'd worried about him and it certainly wasn't good for team spirit that the captain had been left behind. I don't believe, however, as some do, that it was an attempt to sabotage our chances of winning the World Cup. They were just bandits who wanted to make money.

We knew that if we were to win the World Cup our biggest threat would come from Brazil, who were in our group along with Romania and Czechoslovakia. West Germany and Italy were our other major challengers.

We were based initially in Guadalajara and I shared a room with Jack Charlton and my City teammate Francis Lee. Our room was on something like the 102nd floor of the Hilton Hotel.

Memories of my early experience of travelling to Turkey with City came flooding back. About three or four cars of Brazilian fans spent the whole night driving around the hotel playing drums, loud music and standing on bonnets, banging on the cars and basically making as much noise as possible.

Jack got so frustrated about his sleep being interrupted that he threw a bucket of water at them out of the bedroom window. We were that high up that by the time the water reached the ground it had disappeared. Francis and I just kept quiet and tried to sleep.

The following day, Gordon Banks made his much-replayed wonder save against Pelé. I came on as a substitute in that game. It was the first time substitutes had been allowed in the finals. It was a wonderful feeling to be involved in a match of such importance and to be surrounded by great players on both teams.

I started the third game in the group stage, a 1–0 win against the Czechs thanks to a penalty from Allan Clarke.

Back in England, the press made a big issue about the substitutions made by Alf Ramsey. I'd started on the bench for our biggest games against Brazil and then West Germany in the quarter-finals. Some were suggesting that my introduction had a negative effect on the team's performance, pinpointing the moment I came on to replace Bobby Charlton as the mistake that cost us the game. I'm sick of reading that just after I went on Germany scored their first goal, with us leading 2–0 at the time. I was warming up on the touchline with Norman Hunter when the first German goal went in.

In my opinion, just like in the game against Brazil, Alf made the change five minutes too late. He was right to make the changes but the timing was wrong. Several reports suggested that Bobby Charlton was keeping the German captain Franz Beckenbauer occupied and that it was because he took Bobby off that the game changed.

Beckenbauer actually scored that first German goal and I didn't replace Bobby until two minutes later. If Alf had put the substitutes on earlier, it might have been different.

What people forget is that Geoff Hurst had a goal disallowed in extra time; perhaps that was more significant and proved to be the turning point. The substitution of me for Bobby certainly hadn't been pre-planned. Bobby was totally drained when he came off. He was never the type who would coast through a game; he always gave everything he had. He was in the engine room, always wanting to be involved.

The weather had been particularly humid and there was no chance of having a drink. Unlike today, when players take every opportunity to stop the game to top up their fluids, it wasn't allowed then.

I've seen a clip since on TV of Bobby coming back through an airport saying it was a mistake to take him off. That must have been how he felt at the time. I still maintain that the game was falling apart before I went on, not *because* I went on. We lost the game 2–3.

Bobby recently told me, 'No one ever said to me that you were to blame for that defeat. We lost because, defensively, we gave them opportunities we shouldn't have done. For England to concede three goals against anyone was unheard of. Alf took me off on a regular basis – after all, I was about 34 years old. I must admit I was disappointed about coming off at the time because I still felt full of running, but the mistakes that led to the goals we conceded were definitely nothing to do with you.'

Bobby Charlton is my sporting hero. I always judge a player by assessing how many assets he has to his game from my list of 20 playing strengths. In my opinion, Bobby had most of them: beating people, awareness, use of both feet, scoring and making goals and being a team player. I feel privileged to have competed against him a few times and also to have played alongside him for England.

Bobby and I grew up in the North-east of England and I feel there are similarities in our personalities, both being relatively quiet by nature. My admiration for him completely centres on what he did on the park. He remains *my* number one.

Brazil went on to win the World Cup, beating Italy in the final. That Brazilian team is regarded by many as the greatest of all time. One thing's certain, though, Pelé, Rivalino, Jairzinho and the rest were certainly glad to see us eliminated. I believe we could have gone on to beat Brazil if we'd beaten West Germany. We knew we had a really good chance of winning the World Cup and to be 2–0 up in the quarter-final against Germany and lose 2–3 was hard to take.

Chelsea's Peter Bonetti had played in goal because Gordon Banks had food poisoning. That's another conspiracy theory that's never been cleared up. Had someone put something in his food? In the end, I don't think it would have mattered who'd been our goalkeeper that day. Uwe Seeler scored the type of goal he could never have repeated. He was facing away from goal when the ball just seemed to strike him on the head and loop over Bonetti into our goal. It was just meant to be: fate.

Returning from Mexico was one of the worst feelings I had in football. We all felt very low, with Alf particularly deflated. There was a great feeling of anti-climax since we'd set out with such optimism. There were no fans waiting to meet us at the airport when we arrived back, earlier than we'd planned. It took weeks to eradicate a feeling of emptiness from my system.

There was one major benefit from the trip to Mexico. Pre-season training that summer back at City was the easiest I ever knew. I watch athletics on the TV and enjoy the sport generally. If I was a coach or an athlete now, I would go and train at altitude. I was never as fit as when I came back from Mexico. We'd been there for about six weeks altogether and I'm sure I could have run a mile in under four minutes at that time.

Malcolm used to pair us off at Wythenshawe Park, with the best two runners together and then the next best, and so on. He wanted the pairs to be evenly matched, so he paired me with Frank Carrodus, who mainly played in the reserves at that time. He'd have been fresher than me because reserve-team football is never as competitive as playing in the first team. Frank used to be as quick as greased lightning at sprinting and could run all day at three-quarters pace.

At one particular session, Malcolm made us run last. I've no doubt he did that because he thought, for some reason, that it would benefit the rest of the lads. The day's training had been spent near the oval athletics track and he started Frank and me at the proper start line. He wanted us to do a lap and a half. I believed I could beat Frank but he was an excellent runner, so I knew it could prove painful. As soon as Malcolm shouted 'go', off went Frank. It was like the traps had been opened at a White City greyhound meeting. His plan was to run me into the ground.

After a lap, and it had been a quick lap, he was about four

yards in front of me. The 'engine room' (Doyle, Oakes and Pardoe) were standing at the start line, waiting to go across the middle of the track once we'd passed them. They were barracking me, shouting things like, 'He's got him, he'll not make that up.' Apparently they were having bets on who'd win the race.

I could never stand losing and with everyone watching I was determined that there would be no way that I would be beaten. I eased up alongside him and just edged ahead of him on the home straight to beat him by a couple of yards. I had to work very hard that day, more than normal, though I tried to make it look easier than it actually was.

There hadn't been many changes during the summer of 1970, so it was a familiar club that I returned to. Youngsters like Tony Towers, Derek Jeffries and Willie Donachie were starting to become more involved. What would the new season hold? Could we continue our great run of success?

CHAPTER EIGHT
Life-changing Decisions

The 1970–71 season started well, for me personally and for the team. We won six of our opening eight games, in which I scored five goals, and I felt I was playing as well as ever. Our one disappointment during that period was an early exit from the League Cup, at Carlisle United. They were a competitive lower league side and it was a tough, physical game. We played them on a heavy pitch but we still should have been good enough to win.

We were also defending the European Cup-Winners' Cup and started with two games against Linfield from Northern Ireland. Our form clearly suffered in the knockout competitions and we had to rely on the away goals rule to progress to the next round. A more convincing winning margin of 3–0 on aggregate followed against the Hungarian club Honved.

The first leg in Budapest was played in the afternoon, because it was being shown on national TV. The crowd was only small and there was no atmosphere in the stadium. Just under 30,000 were at Maine Road for the second leg, which I remember quite clearly because I was kicked in the head by their right winger, Sandor Pinter, which left me unconscious for a few moments, though eventually I was able to carry on.

We hadn't needed to decide the tie with penalties but if we had, I was one of the players nominated to take one. My previous record included missing one at school and another for Horden Juniors, and from that moment on I was determined never to take another. I was lucky with City, because I never had to take one in a penalty shoot-out. Both those childhood spot-kicks were half-hit shots, with the keeper saving in both cases. I'd aimed both to the goalkeeper's left, the weaker side for a right-handed keeper.

I always looked forward to playing in the derby games against Manchester United. I didn't really know any of the United players on a personal level but I certainly admired the likes of Best, Law and, of course, my hero, Bobby Charlton. United always dominated the headlines, no matter what *we* achieved. They've always been more famous worldwide than City. It probably started as a consequence of the Munich air disaster but whenever I went abroad everybody knew Bobby Charlton and the United team was instantly recognisable.

When I look in the record books at the results during the six to eight years when they had Best, Law and Charlton, and we had our great team at City, we were the top dogs. Most of the time we turned them over! We were simply the better side.

I once had the chance, indirectly, to move to Old Trafford. My friend, Paul Doherty, was chatting to their great manager Sir Matt Busby on a train to London and he asked Paul if I wanted to join United. He told me about it later but I never took the suggestion seriously because, as far as I was concerned, Manchester City was my club. I was 100 per cent happy with everything, so I had no reason to consider moving elsewhere, let alone United.

The situation couldn't have been better for me at City, whether it be on the playing side, the standard of players I was with, the club or the supporters. When you're happy, you perform well and I couldn't have been happier. There was also talk in the *Manchester Evening News* that Real Madrid were interested in signing me. I don't know if there was ever any truth behind the story but I wouldn't have gone even if they'd asked. I didn't want to go abroad and I didn't see any real difference in status between the clubs.

Money had never been my priority, so even if the wages had been higher I wouldn't have been tempted to move. I had a contract, too, and my attitude was that if you signed a contract for three years, that meant you'd be at that club for three years, end of story. I didn't want to be anything but a Manchester City player.

The Old Trafford derby on 12 December 1970 was a significant game for a number of reasons. Most importantly, I'd contacted Marie, the girl I'd met at the Portland Lodge before going to the World Cup, and the evening after the game was to be our first proper date. On the football side, after a good start to the season, we'd only won two of the eleven league games leading up to the fixture, so we needed a victory to put us back on track.

It proved to be Wilf McGuinness's last game as Manchester United manager, with Sir Matt Busby subsequently returning for a short second spell in charge until the end of the season. We won the game convincingly, 4–1. Mike Doyle, who enjoyed beating United more than most, scored the opener and Franny scored a hat-trick.

It was to be a sad day too, with my great friend Glyn Pardoe suffering a broken leg after a challenge by George Best. After the match, I went to be with him in hospital, despite my date with

Marie. I rang her to explain that we couldn't go out that evening and to tell her about Glyn's injury. I called at her parents' house on my way home from hospital to apologise.

It was a bad injury and Glyn never fully recovered from the incident. He played again but missed the whole of the following season as he battled to regain full fitness.

My relationship with Marie survived that missed date, and our courtship soon started in earnest. I was still living in digs with Mrs Girling in Whitefield, while Marie was much more up-market, living in a large house in Hale with her parents.

Marie comes from a middle-class background, her family weren't mega-rich but they were above average. She had a Lotus Elan sports car and was successful in her own right. Nothing I did on the football field impressed her and she had no interest in my 'working life'. She told me, as our relationship developed, that some of the young girls who visited her in the hair salon had admitted they'd got pictures of me on their bedroom walls. We *both* found that hard to understand.

I used to travel to Hale to see her regularly but didn't feel it was right that I went inside the house – because I was always wearing jeans and it didn't seem appropriate. I'd stand there on the doorstep for hours and chat with her before going home again. I had plenty of confidence on the football pitch but lacked self-confidence away from it.

I've never been a person who shows my emotions easily. I don't know if it is a consequence of the changing circumstances of my early years, first living with 'Mum' and then moving to Dad's but I've never been a tactile person. Even when I scored a crucial goal in an important game, I was the type who just ran back to the halfway line, without the histrionics of today's players. I wasn't one of those who hugged and kissed my teammates at every opportunity.

Our emphatic win against United at Old Trafford, followed by an equally convincing victory at Burnley, had only a transient effect on our league form. We won two out of the next three, before going ten games without a win. However, we were still in Europe and in early March 1971 we travelled to Poland to face the team we'd beaten in the final a year earlier, Gornik Zabrze.

The weather there was a few degrees below freezing. As we were playing, they were clearing the touchlines of snow with big shovels made of boards. They left the snow resting on the main surface because it was better to play on that than the frozen pitch that lay beneath. We lost the game 0–2.

As if that wasn't bad enough, the journey home proved to be a bit of a marathon, to say the least. It took a couple of hours to reach the airport by coach, where there were two planes waiting, one for the official party and the other for the supporters. It was a vile night. I don't know how much snow had fallen but I knew one thing – you couldn't see the runway.

We all quickly boarded our plane, eager to go home. Eventually the plane started to inch hesitantly forwards. It was moving more slowly than my first car journey back to the North-east when I'd just passed my driving test! It seemed like we trundled along for about 20 minutes, going around in circles, before we ended up back at our starting point next to the terminal building.

The pilot had apparently taken a trial run looking for 'terra firma', making sure there was something solid underneath the snow. On the second attempt, we followed the tracks from the first run before eventually taking off, much to everyone's relief. The supporters weren't quite as fortunate. The second plane was grounded for the night because it was too dangerous for them to take off.

When I look back on the incident now, it seems quite frightening but at the time we were just relieved to be on the way home. On another European trip, there were a couple of fire engines driving alongside our plane as we came in to land at Manchester Airport. The plane supposedly had a problem with one of its engines. I don't remember being as bothered as I should have been because we'd had a couple of glasses of champagne during the flight.

We won the second leg of the tie with Gornik 2–0, making it 2–2 on aggregate, which meant that a third deciding game had to be played at a neutral venue. The match was played in Copenhagen and we won 3–1 to secure our place in the semi-finals. I couldn't take part in the dressing-room celebrations because I was asked to produce a urine sample.

I was always nervous before games, so, as usual, I'd been to the toilet at regular intervals, passing water up to half a dozen times. Sometimes, I'd be in there every ten minutes. That caused me a problem after the game in Copenhagen because Derek Jeffries and I were required to provide samples. Random drug testing had recently been introduced.

While the rest of the players headed for the dressing-room, we were ushered into a separate room where you could have heard a pin drop, it was so quiet. I'd not had a drink at half-time and found it difficult to produce a sample. Derek took about an hour to oblige but it took me two hours as I was totally dehydrated. By the time I'd finished, all I could do was collect my suit and go straight to the bus where the rest of the players were waiting. I ended up having my shower back at the hotel.

Chelsea were our opponents in the semi-finals. I was unable to play in either of the games against them because of an injury I'd sustained at Newcastle. We lost the tie 0–2 on aggregate, which was a major disappointment. We had a few other injury problems at that time, so it was a severely weakened team that lost to Chelsea.

There were all sorts of internal politics going on at the club during this period, too. There were changes in the boardroom and Malcolm was demanding a bigger role at the club. At one stage he was briefly relieved of his duties but Joe Mercer said that he'd resign if Malcolm went and he was reinstated. The season finished with a 3–4 defeat to United at Maine Road. A season that had held such promise had ended in disappointment.

From a football perspective, it was a terrible summer. I couldn't play for England due to my earlier injury. But away from football, my relationship with Marie was becoming ever stronger and the injury meant we could spend more time together. I always felt she was something special but I didn't understand what attracted her to me.

I used to spend a large part of my spare time with my cousin Roland and his wife Jean. They lived on the same estate as me in Bury. I told Roland and Jean that Marie's parents had a butler who would announce the arrival of guests at the door. They believed every word, which meant they were petrified when they eventually visited the house themselves.

The occasion in question came later in the year when Roland and Jean were invited there to celebrate our engagement. They were worried sick until they realised I'd been joking.

Our engagement on 20 October 1971 was a very special day in my life. The proposal was very traditional. I popped the question at Marie's house, doing everything the way it should be done. Her father was washing up in the kitchen and I think her mum had gone to bed. I'd asked Marie already and she told me that I needed to ask her dad for his permission.

I tried to handle it all in a very matter-of-fact way but of course I was shaking like a leaf, though trying not to show it. I said, 'Jack, I've just asked Marie to marry me and she told me to clear it with you.' He simply replied, 'That's fine,' and continued drying the dishes. I don't think he even looked up; he just carried on like it was an everyday occurrence. I couldn't quite believe it and went straight back to Marie and said, 'I think he said yes!'

My dad, my sister Eileen and her husband Bart, plus Roland and Jean were invited to Marie's parents' home in Hale for the engagement party a few weeks later. Roland and Jean eventually saw the funny side and, of course, Marie's parents didn't really have a butler!

I had a business interest by now, too. I'd continued my friendship with my former Bury teammate Colin Waldron and on the advice of Paul Doherty, the journalist who'd recommended me to Malcolm Allison during my days at Gigg Lane, we bought a coffee bar with an upstairs restaurant in Whitefield. We were trying to plan for our futures and took out loans to buy the business. I think it cost about £25,000 between us, which was a lot of money in those days. We called it the Bell Waldron.

In the beginning, I didn't spend much time there as I was too busy with my football and private life. However, as my fame grew, the supporters expected me to be there to entertain them, so I went to the restaurant when I could.

Initially, I wasn't comfortable in my new role as host. I've never found it easy to walk up to people and introduce myself. I'm not the best of mixers but Paul told me I needed to go round the tables and ask the customers if they were enjoying their meals. Colin Waldron was much better at that sort of thing than I was. I never liked to interrupt people in the middle of their meals, when they were out socialising, so I tended to talk to them as they came in or after they'd finished.

Paul used to get frustrated with me. He suggested that I consult an expert who would help me feel at ease in the company of others and coach me to speak in front of a small audience. I never did act on his advice. I was too scared to go in the first place! One thing that did give me more confidence was drink. I wasn't a heavy drinker but the odd glass would give me a bit of Dutch courage.

'Doc', as I've always called Paul Doherty, tells a few stories about my exploits with drink.

'Colin is not a big drinker, that's for sure, but I remember one night when my wife, Colin, local businessman Tony Brown and I sat around a table playing a game which involved picking a different drink and downing it in one. We were knocking back everything you could think of. By the end of the night, it was crazy. Colin stood up and just keeled over, flat on his face. I had to carry him, with my wife, into my car.

'We drove him to his digs, which were about a mile away. We left the window open all the way and he travelled with his head hanging out of it. Can you imagine what it must have looked like to people walking along the footpath, seeing Colin Bell throwing up down the outside of my car?

'Another time, I took him into Manchester after a busy night at the Bell Waldron and as I drove through a set of traffic lights, a police car pulled me over. I had to take a breathalyser test. It was clear, so the policeman decided to book me for going through a red light, which I immediately denied. I ended up in court.

'My star witness was Colin Bell. I can't think of another professional footballer with so much integrity. He's as straight as a die. Typically, he was brief and to the point, simply explaining that I had not gone through a red light.

'The judge asked how he could be so sure, so Colin quietly explained that he was such a good footballer that he could judge exactly when he'd arrive at a certain point to receive a pass. He stated with confidence that he could easily tell that we hadn't passed through a red light. The case was thrown out.

'That was one of the few times when I saw Colin speak in public without fear. Generally, I felt Colin used to hide behind the bar at the restaurant so he didn't have to meet the punters. He was so shy that it was always a struggle for him to talk to people. It was his name that "made" the restaurant, though Colin Waldron put far more hours into it in the early days because he could mix with the diners more easily.'

Well, I can't really argue with those words from my loyal friend, Doc. I've always thought it strange that people want to meet me or speak to me. I'm just a miner's son from Hesleden. I'm still the same person who grew up in those humble surroundings in County Durham.

CHAPTER NINE
Changes

The summer of 1971 was full of uncertainty. I was recovering from the cartilage injury that had seen me carried off at Newcastle in mid-April and there were various power struggles ongoing, with Malcolm Allison wanting to be the manager. There were changes in the boardroom, too, with Peter Swales becoming a director.

I was being treated at the Manchester Royal Infirmary in the bed next to Mike Doyle, who was also recovering from injury. Most of my time was spent concentrating on playing again and I avoided any involvement in the behind-the-scenes politics at my club.

My cartilage problem required a long time to resolve and it took me until the fifth game of the new season to return to action. I wasn't the only one trying to regain full fitness. Glyn Pardoe was still recovering from the broken leg he'd suffered at Old Trafford, so at least I was in good company. Regrettably, Glyn was forced to sit out the whole of that season.

I scored during my comeback game, a 4–0 win against Spurs

at Maine Road, and was simply happy to be playing again. During the close season, striker Wyn Davies had joined us from Newcastle United. Maine Road itself was changing, too, with new terracing in the North Stand. More significantly, though, Malcolm took over as team manager in October, with Joe becoming general manager.

As ever, my only concern was playing football and although we'd been knocked out of the League Cup by Bolton, we were making good progress in the league. When United visited Maine Road on 6 November, it proved to be a classic derby, although it would have been better if we'd won!

Over 63,000 witnessed a 3–3 draw, with Mike Summerbee's late equaliser earning us a deserved point. Sammy McIlroy was making his debut for United and Wyn Davies was playing in his first derby. We were 0–2 down due to goals from McIlroy and Brian Kidd just after half-time and we had it all to do.

Our side had great character and wouldn't be beaten without a fight. We were soon level, thanks to a penalty from Franny, who then set me up to score the equaliser. John Aston's shot, deflected past Joe Corrigan by Alan Gowling, gave them the lead again but we weren't finished. With just a couple of minutes remaining, Summerbee hit a terrific rising shot past Stepney into the top corner. We'd rescued a draw from one of the most exciting derbies I played in.

Whatever the rights and wrongs of the new management structure at the club, everything was going well. There weren't many changes from the team that had won the championship in 1968. Joe Corrigan was now in goal, Willie Donachie had replaced the injured Glyn Pardoe, Tommy Booth had succeeded George Heslop in defence and Ian Mellor and Tony Towers were sharing the role previously occupied by Tony Coleman.

Perhaps the most surprising change was Wyn Davies for Neil

Young. Youngy left us to join Preston in January 1972. In my opinion, Neil never received the full credit he deserved for his part in our success. The media had always focused on Franny, Mike and me. Neil Young was just as important and I was sorry to see him go.

It was about this time that I was asked to go down to London to film a TV advert for Kellogg's Frosties. Paul Doherty organised it and, against my better judgement, I agreed to take part. How I built up the confidence to do it, I'll never know. It's the only advert I've ever done and I've not done anything remotely similar since. Doc and I travelled down the day before and stayed in a hotel. He knew me well enough to know that I'd probably not sleep very well the night before, so he took me out to a club to help me relax.

He went to the bar and returned with an unopened bottle of brandy. I think I only drank a couple of glasses. He must have had the rest because the following day he was so hungover that I ended up going to the filming on my own. His plan had been to settle my nerves for a good night's sleep, which had worked only too well, in his case.

I spent the whole morning being filmed from every conceivable angle, performing the same routine over and over again. I've no idea how I survived, I was like a rabbit caught in the headlights. I felt like a fool but I still wanted to be a perfectionist in front of the camera. The trouble was I had to imagine I was looking at Tony the Tiger, their cartoon character mascot, who was supposed to be right next to me.

I was only in my early 20s and I was supposed to do a deep growl, which was proving difficult because I had quite a high-pitched voice. I was there for a couple of hours trying to growl these words out. I never lived it down.

The advert hit the TV screens the following year, about the

time we played a game at Plymouth. I could hear people in the crowd shouting, 'Have you brought Tony along? Where's Tony the Tiger?' I certainly took some stick for a few weeks after that. I wasn't the only one performing on screen with Tony the Tiger at that time; the wrestler Mick McManus starred in an advert, too. Even now, I am called by TV companies every so often who want to use it. My answer is always a very definite no!

In the same year, I was also persuaded to take part in the recording of 'Boys in Blue', the song written by Godley and Crème of the pop group 10cc. The whole City team went to Strawberry Studios in Stockport. Singing has never been my strong point – although I did appear on *Top of the Pops* singing 'Back Home', the England anthem for the Mexico World Cup.

I'm still waiting for my gold disc following the success of 'Back Home', which remained at number one for a few weeks. Nevertheless, I think it's fair to say that my singing is better suited to the bathroom.

By the middle of March 1972, we were four points clear at the top of the table and although we'd made a disappointing exit from the FA Cup at Middlesbrough, we believed we could win the championship. Our football was flowing brilliantly and we were playing together as a team. Everyone knew their role and everyone was playing their part.

With nine games remaining in the title race, Malcolm signed Rodney Marsh from Queens Park Rangers for £200,000. He made his debut immediately, in the 1–0 win against Chelsea. After that, he played in seven of the eight remaining games and we won just three times.

I believe it was the arrival of Rodney that season that cost us the league, and Marshy would probably hold his hands up and admit that now, with hindsight. When he was at QPR, I used to nip downstairs on Saturday nights at the Bell Waldron to watch him on *Match of the Day*. I used to love being entertained by Marshy because that's what he was, an entertainer; but he wasn't a City player.

His arrival ruined our game for a while because everything we worked on was based on a one-touch or two-touch basis. I was used to making runs and doing certain types of things, knowing the ball would keep moving on and I would receive passes at certain times. We all knew how the system worked.

Unfortunately, once Rodney was involved he'd take three or four unnecessary touches, beating one player and then another. Playing one-touch football wasn't the way he did things. Malcolm used to tell us to knock the ball in as soon as we had gained a half-yard advantage on our opponent. The onus was then on the forwards to get on the end of the crosses and *they'd* be in trouble if they weren't there at the right time.

Marshy would receive the ball on the left-hand side, reach the line with a half-yard advantage but then check back and play it again before going back towards the line again to beat his opponent for a second time. All this time, while he was down by the corner flag, we'd be running into the box, coming out and then going back in again. After a few times, we'd stop making runs, at which time he'd finally deliver the cross, but of course there was no one there to meet it. We all ended up looking foolish.

He wasn't a Manchester City type of player. It wasn't Marshy's fault. In training, he was one of the best there was, he couldn't have made any more effort. He was always in the leading group when we did cross-country running or sprinting and he had a warm personality. His style of football just didn't suit the way we'd been doing things at Maine Road.

Rodney has always had bags of confidence and was the self-proclaimed king of 'head tennis', a game we played during training. There was a net in the gym and you had to kick or head the ball over it and it was only allowed to bounce once on each side. Rodney used to boast that he was unbeatable. Not much used to get to me but one day, egged on by some of my teammates and our physiotherapist Freddie Griffiths, I decided to take Rodney on.

Everyone went quiet as we entered the gym for the duel. I didn't say much, I never did, but I was determined to show him he was getting too big for his boots. I think I beat him 5–0, 5–0, 5–0. After the match, I simply shook his hand, changed and went home. I'd done what I wanted to do; no words were required. When something made me angry, the only way I knew how to express my feelings was with my football boots on.

I used to argue with referees all the time. I never swore, though. I'd hound referees and argue for every throw, every free-kick and anything else I thought should have gone our way. Where others would swear, I'd use words like 'ruddy' or 'flippin' but never anything worse than that. People who know that I don't swear have asked me if it's because I'm deeply religious or something like that. The simple answer is that I just don't see, and have never seen, the need to swear.

Although we beat United 3–1 at Old Trafford during the run-in that season, with two goals from Franny and one from Rodney, we ended the campaign in fourth place, just one point behind the champions, Derby County. What a disappointment; but worse was yet to follow.

During the summer of 1972, the Mercer–Allison partnership was broken up with Joe moving to Coventry City and Malcolm taking sole control. I always felt the pair had complemented each other perfectly. Joe was the father figure and always gave good advice. Everyone adored him but he was relatively quiet. Malcolm was the extrovert and had a great coaching brain. He was the best there was. It was truly the end of a great era when the pair split up.

The domestic season might have ended but there was plenty to keep me busy. My wedding to Marie that summer was fast approaching and there was still plenty to do on the football pitch.

The European Nations Cup wasn't the huge tournament it is today, and England still hadn't qualified for the much more modest final stages. We had to beat West Germany over two legs to qualify but we lost out to them again, as we'd done in Mexico, leaving just the home internationals to bring the season to an end.

As was the norm in those days, England played the three home countries, Scotland, Wales and Northern Ireland, over a one week period. All the players who participated were awarded a single commemorative cap, with the three opponents' names stitched in a panel above the peak. For normal one-off internationals we'd receive an individual cap for that game, with the opponent's name embroidered beneath the three lions badge.

Some of my England caps are still unopened. They arrive in what looks like a cake box, surrounded by soft tissue paper. The different coloured tassels indicate whether it's for an Under-23 or full international. They're not fitted and come in a standard size. I don't think they're designed to be worn while you're out shopping.

I enjoyed the home internationals. They were great for team building, because the squad came together at the end of every season for a couple of weeks. The danger, at international level, was that the players were relative strangers. It takes time to become accustomed to each other's style of play and the home internationals were perfect for that purpose.

The other advantage was that the games were highly competitive, because you played against teammates and opponents from the football league. I found that more interesting and I think the public did, too. The style of football was what you'd expect from four British sides: end-to-end attacking. In Europe, it was more a game of patience, feeling each other out and only attacking occasionally. I believe that the British way is the best.

I captained England once during my career and it was on 23 May 1972 against Northern Ireland at Wembley. I always believed there should be 11 captains in the side, with every player giving or taking advice as needed. There's no point hiding, waiting for someone else to make the decisions.

Tony Book was City's great captain, and a wonderful leader, but if you watch videos of those games you'll see that we all acted as a captain should. I'm not sure why I was appointed skipper against Northern Ireland and it was a one-off because Bobby Moore remained captain for the next year or so. Nevertheless, it was a privilege being asked by Alf Ramsey to take on the role.

The biggest rivalry existed between England and Scotland. Typically, I would never show any emotion but I certainly felt it against Scotland. There were plenty in our dressing-room who spent the last hour before kick-off shouting and bawling and kicking their toe-ends against the walls to get themselves going. The supporters were the same; in fact, the Scottish supporters were frightening.

The games against Scotland at Wembley often felt like away games. On the way to Hampden Park that year, a Scottish fan bounced a bottle off one of the windows of our coach. They'd obviously been drinking, which made it even more difficult to predict what they were going to do. My favourite win against Scotland was during the summer of 1972. Alan Ball scored the only goal to give us a 1–0 victory.

The atmosphere at England versus Scotland games was better than the cup finals. It was almost like a war. I used to relish the competition against the likes of Billy Bremner, Denis Law and later Kenny Dalglish. They had some great players and on paper their team always looked very strong, though they didn't really click as a team. It's probably a good job they didn't.

Still to come during the summer of 1972 was a moment even better than winning the League Championship, the FA Cup, League Cup or European Cup-Winners' Cup – my wedding to Marie. We were married on a beautiful summer's day at St Peter's Church in Hale village on Thursday, 22 June. My best man was my former Bury teammate John Bain and as many of my friends at City that could make it were in attendance.

Malcolm couldn't come but his first wife Beth was there, along with Summerbee, Doyley, Glyn and Booky. Unfortunately, Oakey was away on holiday, so he was unable to join us. Joe Mercer and his wife Norah were invited, too, although they only came to the church and then made a discreet exit. Joe had recently been sacked by City and didn't want to cause any tension. Dad and his wife, Cissie, came down from Hesleden along with Eileen, Bart and Keith, and Mum brought her daughter Joyce with her.

It was a very special day for all of us and I was pleased to be able to share it with all the people that mattered to me. The service was very traditional, just as our courtship had been. We lived apart until the day we were married, as it should be. The reception was at the Bell Waldron, as Doc had suggested it would be bad PR to hold it anywhere else. It wasn't really big enough but we all managed to squeeze in for a stand-up buffet.

As I was the groom, I had to make a short speech, thanking the bridesmaids and the parents, that sort of thing. I found it a lot easier than the public appearances that were expected from me as Colin Bell the footballer. We went on honeymoon to Nassau in the Bahamas. The whole occasion was perfect and marrying Marie was the best decision I ever made. We even bumped into Bobby Charlton and his wife Norma on our return journey. Could things have been any better?

CHAPTER TEN

Horses For Courses

Off the field, things couldn't have been better. I was starting my married life with the woman I loved and business at the Bell Waldron restaurant was going well. The new football season began on a high, too. Although we had only finished fourth in the First Division, we were invited to compete for the Charity Shield and beat Third Division champions, Aston Villa, 1–0 at Villa Park to give our new manager Malcolm Allison his first trophy.

Malcolm felt that Leeds United would be our biggest rivals to win the title and the bookmakers agreed. Despite my optimism, we didn't start the new league season well, losing five of the opening six games. To make matters worse, we were knocked out of the League Cup at my old club Bury and were beaten 1–2 by Valencia in Spain, in the UEFA Cup. We lost the tie 3–4 on aggregate, to go out of the competition at the first-round stage.

After looking forward to the new season so much, within a couple of months we were bottom of the table and desperately in need of a few victories to climb out of trouble. Wins against

West Ham, Derby and Everton gave us a lift as we approached another derby.

I always looked forward to the Manchester derbies. In total, I played against United twenty-one times during my career, scoring eight goals, which isn't a bad record for a midfielder. Only Joe Hayes and Francis Lee scored more goals in derbies than I did: a record that makes me very proud.

The derby was at Maine Road on 18 November 1972. I remember it being a bad-tempered game at times. My former City colleague Wyn Davies was in their starting line-up. I opened the scoring early in the game with a simple tap-in, following a collision between the United goalkeeper Alex Stepney and his teammate Tony Dunne.

I should have been credited with a hat-trick because I scored the other two goals, too, to win 3–0. However, one of them was recorded as an own goal by Martin Buchan, as it deflected off him en route to goal. It wasn't to be the last time Martin Buchan spoiled my day in a derby.

Away from football, I'd developed a passion for racehorses. My interest in racing started soon after I joined City, when a friend of Malcolm's gave me a horse called Stay Back. Along with Colin Waldron and Paul Doherty, I paid for the horse to be trained by Frank Carr at Malton in North Yorkshire. Frank was one of the best trainers around. Unfortunately, Stay Back lived up to its name and never won a race while under our ownership.

Its biggest chance came in a race at Catterick, when Frank had tipped us off that it was going to do well. I checked the odds in Friday's *Manchester Evening News* and they were at a favourable 100–8, so we backed it with our entire kitty, carefully accumulated over the previous months at £5 a week. The day it ran we were playing at Burnley, so only Doc was able to go and watch the horse at the track.

Doc made the mistake of trying to bet our entire £300 stake with one bookie, which must have sent alarm bells ringing, and within seconds word had spread that the horse was highly fancied. Suddenly, Stay Back was the 13–8 favourite and despite running between the various bookmakers in an attempt to find better odds, he only managed to place a single bet.

We won the match at Burnley 4–0 and I scored twice. On the way home to Manchester, I asked Sid, who drove the team coach, to stop outside a newsagents so I could buy a copy of the *Football Pink* to check the result in the Stop Press section. It only listed the first three horses and Stay Back wasn't one of them. I assumed it had been a printing error. I was convinced the horse would be placed at the very least, especially with the top-quality jockey Martin Blackshaw riding him.

Once Doc returned from the course, he explained that Stay Back had suffered a burst blood vessel halfway round and had been pulled up. We sold the horse after that. A couple of years later, Stay Back eventually won a race at 20–1 but, much to my frustration, I had nothing on it. By now our syndicate had acquired Stay Bell. It was my name, of course, but it also rhymed with 'Stable', which we thought was quite clever!

The others in the syndicate had become my partners at the Bell Waldron. They included Doc and Wally, plus Tony Brown, who was a baker in Whitefield. I'd come to know Tony well, as he was one of our main suppliers at the restaurant.

We went to see Stay Bell run on a number of occasions, with a trip to Ayr being particularly eventful. Doc had borrowed a Rolls-Royce belonging to Ken Bates, who was the chairman of Oldham Athletic. Marie and I were travelling separately when I noticed a car approaching quickly from behind. As the vehicle drew alongside, I realised it was Doc at the wheel. We parked our car in a hotel car park near the Scottish Borders and continued the journey with Doc and Tony Brown, in style, in the Roller.

A racegoer recognised me when we arrived at the course and asked if our horse would win. 'I wouldn't have come all the way from Manchester if I didn't think it would win,' was my quick reply and we moved purposefully into the stands to watch it run.

Stay Bell didn't have a good day and cantered home in last place. As we made our way back to where the Roller was parked, I heard a voice shout out, 'Hey, I thought you said your horse was going to win.' It was the punter I'd spoken to on the way in. I hurried along, trying to blend in with the crowd, embarrassed at Stay Bell's failure. The car seemed a safe haven but as I turned the key in the lock, it snapped in half.

I couldn't open the door and was left there like a groom stood-up at the altar. Obtaining a replacement key or arranging for a locksmith to come from Edinburgh proved time consuming and we ended up going to a hotel in Ayr for something to eat and drink. Eventually, complete with our new key, we returned to the car and set off home at about 11.30 p.m., lessons learnt.

Eventually, Stay Bell became quite successful, though mainly after we'd sold it. Under the ownership of Sir Hugh Fraser, who'd made his fortune from department stores, it won about ten or twelve times over jumps after failing us on the flat. We did have one success with it at Carlisle, although I was abroad at the time. I never actually saw any of my horses win.

After the win, we decided to sell it, thinking that we could demand a better price. I love horses, each with its own personality. Just like people, they can be moody and unpredictable.

I suppose as a football team, we shared those traits at that time and had become inconsistent. By the turn of the year, the

FA Cup seemed our only chance of winning silverware. We started well enough with a 3–2 win against Stoke City.

Malcolm was up to his old tricks in the build-up to our fourth-round tie, suggesting we would 'bury the Liverpool myth' when we faced Bill Shankly's side at Anfield. The psychology seemed to work, because we beat them 2–0 in a replay at Maine Road, with Tommy Booth and me scoring the goals.

When we were drawn at home to Second Division Sunderland in the fifth round, we were rapidly installed as joint favourites with Leeds to win the competition. Bob Stokoe, who'd been the Bury manager when I'd signed for them a decade earlier, was in charge, at the club I'd supported as a boy.

Tony Towers scored an early goal but then a mistake by Joe Corrigan saw his goal-kick towards Willie Donachie intercepted by Micky Horswill, who quickly lobbed the ball over Big Joe's head for the equaliser. Dennis Tueart set Billy Hughes up for their second which meant we had to work very hard just to get a replay.

We were fortunate to take the game back to Roker Park but happily accepted the gift of an own goal when their goalkeeper, Jim Montgomery, punched Mike Summerbee's corner into his own net.

We lost the replay 1–3 and our season seemed to be over. That defeat seemed to knock our confidence and we lost six of the next seven league games. The mood among the players was low. Malcolm was more affected by the slump than anyone and he took the 1–2 home defeat to Coventry City the hardest. Joe Mercer had returned to a hero's welcome and his side had taken the two points.

It proved to be the final straw for Malcolm, who left to join Crystal Palace a few weeks later. Chief coach Johnny Hart was asked to fill the void left by Malcolm and although there was little left to play for, our performances improved and we finished the season in mid-table.

I'd always liked Johnny from the first day I met him down at Lilleshall, just after I'd joined City. If Johnny Hart had a weakness, it was that he was perhaps a bit too nice. He got on well with all the players but I was never convinced he would be the right man to be manager. I thought his best role was as coach, as he had been for many years. I believe in horses for courses.

A difficult season for City had come to an end with another change of manager. I'd been used to continuity during my early years at City and I can't deny that I felt a little uneasy about the changes that seemed to be happening all the time. I've always been self-motivated and was determined not to let circumstances beyond my control affect me.

I had the consolation of knowing that the England set-up was the same as ever. Alf Ramsey, the World Cup-winning manager, was the foundation, and there was every indication that we would be going to the finals in West Germany in a year's time. It would be my second chance to play in the best tournament in the world. We were well into our qualifying campaign when we travelled to Poland in June 1973.

There were three teams in our group: England, Wales and Poland. We'd started the group well with a win in Wales and I'd scored the goal. Only the group winners would go through to the finals, where we would be one of the favourites to win the tournament, as we had been in Mexico.

We were expecting to win in Poland, or at least draw, and things seemed to be going to plan in the early stages. I felt we were marginally the better side until Bobby Moore made an uncharacteristic mistake, giving the Poles a chance from which they scored to take the lead. We lost the game 0–2 but knew that if we beat them in the return game at Wembley later in the year, we would still qualify.

England had one more game to play against the USSR. I travelled to Moscow for the friendly but soon after arriving I received a call from home informing me that Marie was unwell. She was five months pregnant and I was told there was a danger she could lose the baby.

Alf asked me to see him and before I could say anything he was instructing me to go home to be with my wife. I rushed to Marie's side but could do nothing to help. Marie lost the baby, a girl, and we were both devastated.

I have never been one to seek publicity nor do I enjoy reading about myself in the newspapers. Most of the time I could just ignore it, if I wished, and get on with playing football. However, the interest in my private life, and the loss of our baby in particular, was the one time in my career when press intrusion really became an issue for me. It was bad enough losing our baby without seeing headlines in the papers telling the world of our grief.

When I was a player, I never talked freely about my personal life, even to my teammates. My private life was not something to be shared with others and any problems at home were our own, nobody else's. The press coverage threw us into an unwanted spotlight.

Naturally the rest of the summer was spent with Marie, our first as man and wife. We kept out of the public eye and spent a lot of time helping each other come to terms with our loss.

Over the years, she's become a very good cook but during those early days we ate fairly basic cuisine. However, when it comes to cleaning and dusting, she's in a league of her own. Whenever we go on holiday, she does the 'moonwalk', like Michael Jackson, going backwards, cleaning as she goes, until we reach the door.

Most of the time, she won't even let me choose the clothes I'm going to wear. I get up to find everything laid out for me, right down to which socks match the shoes I'm going to wear that day. Although I'd been used to being a leader on the football pitch since being captain of Bury as a teenager, playing second fiddle at home doesn't bother me at all. I'm easy going and prefer the quiet life.

Marie took little interest in my football career. She would have little concern whether I'd played well or badly and would certainly have nothing to say on the matter. Once I walked through the door of our new home, I had escaped from the spotlight, which suited me fine.

I'd spent less time than usual back in Hesleden during the summer of 1973, so when I received a call telling me my dad was in hospital, I didn't appreciate how ill he actually was. Naturally we went to see him but I assumed he would make a full recovery, returning home without any real concern. A few days later, the unexpected news arrived that he had passed away. The date was 29 July 1973.

Marie and I returned to Hesleden for the funeral and I found it hard to let out my emotions. I've never been good at showing people how I feel. I guess I was in shock but the only way I knew how to cope was to keep my feelings in check. I didn't cry. Perhaps it would have been better if I had but somehow I couldn't. It had been a terrible summer and I was glad when the new football season approached, as it gave me something else to focus my attention on.

Unlike my early years at City, the new campaign was a time of great change, not least because the new manager made a few changes to the playing staff. One of Johnny Hart's first signings was Denis Law, who had been allowed to leave United by their manager, Tommy Docherty, on a free transfer. It seemed hard to believe that both Denis Law and Rodney Marsh would be in our team. Only a couple of years earlier I'd enjoyed watching both players on *Match of the Day* and now they were at City.

Rodney had put in a transfer request when Malcolm left but I was glad when he withdrew it during that summer. Despite the disruption he'd caused to the team when he'd signed, I never lacked admiration for his ability and he was undoubtedly a great entertainer.

Denis scored twice against Birmingham City on his second debut for City. He'd played for the club as a youngster, long before he'd made his name at United. I managed to get the other. Our forward line was very impressive that day. I played alongside Mike Summerbee, Francis Lee, Rodney Marsh and Denis Law. Furthermore, it had been a beautiful sunny day and we'd won comfortably and in style.

In our second game of the season, at Derby, Glyn Pardoe returned. He'd only played a few games the previous season as he struggled to recover from the broken leg he'd suffered at Old Trafford two years earlier. Although we lost the game 0–1, having Glyn back was a great lift.

There were changes at boardroom level, too, with Peter Swales taking over as chairman from Albert Alexander. Mr Alexander had been City chairman when I joined the club and I thought he was brilliant, I really liked him. He avoided any involvement in the day-to-day football matters. He just turned up at games, enjoying them as a supporter, and ran the club's finances in the background.

I knew Peter Swales reasonably well, better than most of the other players, because he was a friend of Paul Doherty's. Doc had been involved in his company, White and Swales, in Altrincham. I wouldn't say I was close to Peter Swales – but then again I wouldn't have expected to have a close relationship with the chairman.

As his time at City went along, he became increasingly more involved in the playing side and I didn't agree with that. The chairman should stick to running the club. To me, the football side is completely different and the two jobs should be kept entirely separate.

Although we'd made a reasonable start to the season and were playing some great football, we were still a little inconsistent and our manager, Johnny Hart, was finding it difficult to cope with the expectation that was now on his shoulders. How do you follow Joe Mercer and Malcolm Allison? He didn't talk to us about the pressure he was under but he didn't seem to be enjoying life as much as when he'd been part of Malcolm's coaching staff.

I simply concentrated on playing well in every game and one of my priorities was to help England qualify for the World Cup finals. What a tournament that would be to play in! At 28 years old, I'd be at my peak and might never get a better chance to emulate my great heroes who won the competition in 1966. All we had to do was beat Poland at Wembley.

It was 17 October 1973 and despite losing in Poland everyone expected us to win the return game comfortably. I loved playing under floodlights and prepared for the match in my usual way: a few trips to the toilet and a few butterflies with an underlying expectation of victory.

We started well enough and I thought the football we played that night was as good as it had ever been. The only thing wrong was that we were struggling to score a goal. If I could turn back the clock and play that game again I'd want virtually everything to be the same. We had the right amount of possession and enough chances to win comfortably. We absolutely paralysed them that night and it was the most one-sided international I ever played in.

One of the most talked about incidents was Norman Hunter's tackle, on the halfway line, 12 minutes into the second half. We knew we had to win the game to go through, so Norman was not only trying to win the tackle but keep the ball in play, too.

Normally, he would have kicked the man and the ball into the Royal Box. Even when Norman missed the tackle and Domarski ran clear, you would still have hung your hat on Peter Shilton saving his shot from just outside the box – but not that night.

That goal meant we had to score two. Within a few minutes, we were awarded a penalty. Martin Chivers couldn't watch as the spot-kick was about to be taken by Allan Clarke. Both Martin and I were convinced that Allan would miss because nothing seemed to be going right for us but he coolly scored to level things at 1–1.

Perhaps we could still win. We laid siege to their goal but just couldn't create a winner. Brian Clough, who'd just resigned as manager of Derby County, labelled the Polish goalkeeper, Jan Tomaszewski, 'The Clown' on TV but he certainly wasn't a clown that night. He was inspired. He saved them with his shins, his forearms and every other part of his body. We hit the post, the bar and defenders on the line. We did everything but score.

Normally, I was the type of player who spent most of the 90 minutes running from one end of the pitch to the other. That night, I spent most of my time in their half and had several shots that were stopped, one way or another. It finished 1–1 and we were out of the World Cup.

Failing to beat Poland and losing out on a World Cup finals place was the biggest disappointment of my career. I was always a bad loser and while it would normally take three or four days for me to get over a defeat with City, this was much worse. World Cups only come round every four years and I'd mainly been a substitute in Mexico, so this had been my big chance.

I remember Alf Ramsey telling us that the squad of 1974 was better than the one that had won it in 1966. Alf wasn't one to make statements just for the sake of it. He was a good manager and a good motivator, though the press didn't seem to take to him. He only spoke to them when he had to, preferring to concentrate on working with the team. He was a 'player's man', putting a lot of thought into the games and handling all of us very well as individuals. He didn't shout and bawl at us; he treated us like men.

One incident that summed up his priorities was when the players were targeted by one of the major boot suppliers. We were being offered more money to play in their boots than we were getting paid to actually play for England. Naturally, we agreed to wear their new boots and we all ended up limping around with blisters after training in them. Alf was furious that we'd put commercial concerns ahead of the success of the team. He was right, too.

The result against Poland put great pressure on Alf and many of the newspapers called for him to resign. He was eventually sacked the following spring – and it didn't go down well with the players. I liked the way Alf did things and it wasn't his fault we hadn't beaten Poland; it was just bad luck.

CHAPTER ELEVEN
New Beginnings

Johnny Hart's health suffered from the moment he accepted the manager's job at City. He hadn't wanted to let anyone down but he'd already had medical problems before he succeeded Malcolm Allison. By November, he was in hospital complaining of complete numbness down one side of his body. He clearly couldn't continue, so the new chairman, Peter Swales, took the opportunity to make a big change by appointing the former Norwich City manager, Ron Saunders, as our new boss.

I wasn't familiar with Ron, so I didn't know what to expect from him but first impressions were not good. As far as I was concerned, he didn't do himself any favours when he came in wielding the axe from day one. One of the first people he sent packing was chief scout Harry Godwin, who'd brought so many good players to the club and had been a father-figure to many of us.

If you're going to make unpopular decisions, then they have to be carried out in the right way. I felt that he upset a lot of people by handling things so bluntly from the moment he

TOP: Me (front row left) as an 11 year old with East Durham Under-15s in 1957.

LEFT: My first photo as a professional footballer, with Bury in 1963.
(© Colorsport)

ABOVE: The scene in the dressing-room after winning the League Championship at Newcastle on 11 May 1968. (© PA/EMPICS)

BELOW: The 'all-conquering' 1969–70 squad with trophies.
(© PA/EMPICS)

ABOVE: Alf gives me a consoling pat on the back after our defeat by West Germany in Mexico. (© Colorsport)

BELOW: The proudest day of my life, 22 June 1972, the day I married Marie. (© *Manchester Evening News*)

LEFT: Bobby Charlton, Alf Ramsey and I discuss tactics over tea. (© Popperfoto)

BELOW: (l–r) Mike Summerbee, me, Rodney Marsh, Wyn Davies, Francis Lee and Malcolm Allison see the funny side. (© *Manchester Evening News*)

RIGHT: England manager Joe Mercer presents me with the Footballer of the Month trophy for May 1974.

ABOVE: Roy Bailey (left) and Freddie Griffiths help carry me off after
my terrible injury at Maine Road in November 1975.
(© *Manchester Evening News*)

BELOW: Best, Law and Charlton meet Bell, Lee and
Summerbee at the launch of our videos in 1990.

LEFT: Seven of the best, including: League Cup winner's trophy, 100 League Legends medal, Second Division Championship medal, First Division Championship medal, FA Cup winner's medal and European Cup-Winners' Cup winner's medal.
(© Kevin Cummins)

BELOW: Cliff Richard, me, Greg Rusedski and my son Jon after a charity tennis event for the Lorna Fogarty Trust.
(© Jean Havillard)

RIGHT: My daughter Dawn graduating in maths at Oxford in 1996.

LEFT: My son Jon graduating in medicine at St Andrews in 2000.

ABOVE: Official opening of the Colin Bell Stand, with Kevin Keegan and supporters from the Yeovil Branch, in February 2004.
(© Ed Garvey)

BELOW: The family with my MBE in the grounds of Buckingham Palace in April 2005. (Photo by Charles Green)

arrived at City. I thought a lot of Harry and felt he deserved more respect. We were a family club and Harry was loved and was doing a great job. I felt Ron Saunders was wrong to treat him that way.

Very quickly, there were plenty of comings and goings among the players, too. Ron was not only making changes but he was rubbing people up the wrong way. It was clear to me from the beginning that he was never going to make it work.

The defenders were especially discontented. Willie Donachie in particular used to look depressed when he came in from training. There was no room for debate with Ron Saunders; he wanted everything done his way. If you didn't fall into line, he wanted rid of you. For some reason, he didn't really interfere with the midfield, so I didn't have any specific incidents with him but I could feel the change in atmosphere and it wasn't good for the club.

Hardly surprisingly, our form in the league and the cup competitions remained inconsistent. Having beaten Walsall in the League Cup, after two replays, we won at Carlisle and then put four past York City, in a replay, to advance to the quarter-finals. The FA Cup had also started well, with a 5–2 win at Oxford before a fourth-round tie at Nottingham Forest.

The match was played at the City Ground on a Sunday afternoon, during the miners' strikes. I remember Duncan McKenzie running us ragged. McKenzie was an entertainer with great skill and he orchestrated the game, with my former teammate Ian Bowyer scoring a couple of their goals. We lost 1–4, proving conclusively that we were not a Sunday-league team!

Although we were below halfway in the league, we still had hope in the League Cup. We progressed through to the semi-finals by beating Coventry City 4–2 in a muddy replay at Maine

Road. We'd been 1–2 down at one stage but battled back to earn a place in the last four. That match, just like the FA Cup tie at Forest, had been affected by the miners' strikes, being played on a Wednesday afternoon because of the power cuts.

We took nothing for granted against Plymouth in the semis, even though they were a Third Division team. After a 1–1 draw at Home Park, we beat them 3–1 at Maine Road. I scored one of the goals with a lob and I remember Franny getting one of the others with a typical thunderbolt of a shot.

The final took place at Wembley on 3 March 1974 and it was to be the only time Marie would see me play live. She only went to the game because there was an organised trip for the wives. I think Marie was more excited about shopping on Oxford Street and Regent Street than she was about watching me play.

The Wembley playing surface was in a much better condition than it had been for our previous finals and despite all the changes that had been made off the field we expected to beat Wolves. Ron Saunders' approach to the big game was very different than it had been under Joe and Malcolm.

Ron was much stricter in his approach and we weren't allowed to drink alcohol during the build-up to the game, not even a glass of wine with our meals. It wasn't as much fun as it had been under Malcolm. It was the only time in my career that I wasn't really happy, as a player, at City.

The game itself reminded me of the Poland match just a few months earlier. Again, we were the dominant side but failed to score. If either of those games had been boxing matches, the opposition would have thrown in the towel long before the end. Wolves took the lead just before half-time, thanks to a volley from Kenny Hibbitt. We went in 0–1 down at half-time but I was still confident we would win the game.

Rodney, Tommy Booth and Franny all had great chances early

in the second half before a cross from Rodney fell kindly into my path and I hit the equaliser past Gary Pierce. With ten minutes of the game remaining, I got the ball on the edge of their box and managed to get a shot away. It hit the underside of the crossbar and bounced out, just like Geoff Hurst's at Wembley in 1966, but unfortunately for me, this time there was no Russian linesman. The more the game went on, the more it felt like the ill-fated World Cup qualifier against Poland.

During the last 30 minutes, we were never out of their half. However, once again I was to leave Wembley broken-hearted, as a late John Richards goal, deflected to him from Rodney's heel, proved to be the winner.

Rodney was badly affected by the defeat, refusing to collect his runners-up tankard. We all shared the great sense of anti-climax; we weren't used to losing cup finals and it was an awful feeling.

Ron Saunders' reaction to losing was to continue with his rebuilding of the team. Dennis Tueart and Mick Horswill joined us from Sunderland, with Tony Towers going the other way. Saunders had taken a dislike to Francis Lee, Mike Summerbee and Denis Law, who he saw as the strong characters who were most likely to stand up to him.

I remember a players' meeting being called on one occasion and I went along to see what was said. They wanted to confront Ron and tell him how we all felt. I was never a person to take the lead in that sort of thing but I agreed with the majority who made it clear they wanted him to adopt a more flexible approach.

I've read allegations that we didn't try in the Maine Road derby on 13 March but they are completely false. I never played in a game for City where the players didn't give it everything they had, especially against United. It is fair to say, though, that we weren't happy with the situation and that could have had a detrimental effect on our performance.

It was a bad-tempered affair, with Mike Doyle and Lou Macari sent off but refusing to leave the field. Referee Clive Thomas had to take both teams off to calm things down before eventually leading us out again – but with both sides reduced to ten men. We drew the game 0–0. United were in relegation trouble and we weren't doing much better.

Chairman Peter Swales sacked Ron Saunders, as it was apparent he'd lost the support of most of the players. He called in some of the more outspoken individuals, like Franny, Mike and Rodney, one by one, and asked them who the players wanted as manager. The verdict was that Tony Book should take over.

Booky had been our captain during the trophy-winning years and was part of the family. He knew us all well and we knew he wouldn't upset the equilibrium. I felt it was a good appointment for Manchester City.

With Booky in command, we earned the points we needed to stay up. We finished the season in 14th place but United were still in trouble at the bottom of the table when we went to Old Trafford for the final match of the season on 27 April 1974. All the hype in the press was that we were trying to relegate United, though in the dressing-room we didn't need any extra motivation to beat them.

I had no sympathy for their position. That's football. I'm sure they would not have had any sympathy for us if the positions had been reversed. Naturally, the spotlight was on Denis Law, who was making his first return to Old Trafford since being given a free transfer the previous summer.

Scotland had qualified for the World Cup finals and Denis was in their squad, having been scoring regularly and playing well. It must have been extremely difficult for Denis to prepare for the derby. I can't imagine how I would have felt if I'd had to play *against* City in such a crucial game. He'd spent most of his career playing at United. It was his club, just like City is my club.

Being the consummate professional, he knew only one way to play and that was to do his job, although he didn't seem to have his heart in it. The atmosphere that day was aggressive. I could feel the anxiety coming from the United supporters and you could tell that their emotions were right on the edge. United needed to win to have a chance of staying up and still needed results elsewhere to go their way.

The goal that decided the match came with just a few minutes to go. I picked up the ball in midfield and ran forward before slipping it out to Francis Lee. Franny crossed low towards the penalty spot, where Denis was standing back to goal, facing away from the Stretford End. Their noisiest and most volatile supporters were standing at that end. Denis reacted instinctively, back-heeling the ball past Stepney. It might have looked a bit casual, like it didn't matter, but it went in.

I was the first to go over to him after he scored and I tried to crack a joke that it wasn't an own goal, pointing out that he'd scored for the right team. I never celebrated much when I scored but I asked him why he was looking so glum as I slapped him playfully on the face. I was pleased, naturally, that we'd scored against United in such a big game against the old enemy.

Denis didn't say anything; he was stunned. Within seconds, Booky brought Phil Henson on as a substitute to replace him. He didn't have the heart to carry on. It proved to be Denis's last kick as a City player. What a way to end a glorious career!

As Denis left the field more and more supporters were encroaching onto the pitch. It had started when he scored, presumably prompted by a few United fans who wanted to console their great hero. Denis had reacted as though somebody had died, rather than with the pleasure I felt inside. I wanted to beat United every time I played against them, though I wouldn't say I wanted them to be relegated. I enjoyed the competition that existed between the two clubs. All I wanted was to beat United home and away every season and for us to be league champions with them below us.

The small sympathetic pitch invasion dispersed quite quickly but a few minutes later there was another invasion from the United fans. This time there was a different atmosphere; much more threatening. We were quickly taken off the pitch by referee David Smith. I was worried that somebody might be hurt in the ensuing chaos and was happy to see all my teammates safely back in the dressing-room. We sat there for a while, wondering what was going on outside.

Eventually, the referee told us that the game would not continue as thousands of supporters remained on the pitch and the police and stewards were having difficultly controlling them. We assumed the result would stand, even though there were still four minutes to play. The result was officially confirmed and we'd won the game 1–0.

Results elsewhere that day went against United anyway and they were relegated. The only thing that mattered to me was that we'd beaten them in the last match of the season, so I could start the summer in a happy frame of mind.

I remember listening to a radio broadcast a few years ago and my ears pricked up when a reporter mentioned that City were playing in a 'derby' game. The match they were referring to was against Stockport County, but I don't class that, without being disrespectful, as a derby. There is only one Manchester derby and that's between City and United.

The summer break was almost upon us, though of course

England were not to be involved in the World Cup. There were, however, the home internationals, a friendly against Argentina and a short tour to Eastern Europe to look forward to.

Joe Mercer had taken charge of England by now, in a caretaker capacity. Joe's team, as ever, reflected his personality and it was a pleasure to be working with him again. It was football with a smile and I was looking forward to the three games against Bulgaria, East Germany and Yugoslavia.

Joe knew he was only a 'stop-gap' manager, which took all the pressure off him and the players. There were a few different faces in the squad by then, too. Duncan McKenzie, Martin Dobson and Malcolm Macdonald had joined the regulars. We did really well at that time and played the sort of football I enjoyed, based on passing and movement and, most of all, attacking. Joe's team talks remained characteristically simple. 'You're a good group of players, be patient and enjoy yourselves.'

We shared the home internationals with Scotland, after winning in Wales, beating Northern Ireland and losing 0–2 in Scotland. Next up was a 2–2 draw at Wembley with Argentina and then we were off to Leipzig to face East Germany.

I was enjoying my football and felt I was playing well, even though we only drew in East Germany and beat Bulgaria by a single goal.

When we arrived in Yugoslavia, the airport seemed dead. Not only were there very few people around but there didn't seem to be much of anything, just a bench to put our bags on to be checked. We all walked on one side of it, because the other side was behind the counter. As Kevin Keegan came in, he walked on the other side of the bench and was immediately stopped and taken away by two burly armed men with guns.

They grabbed him roughly and pushed him through a side

door, away from the rest of us. Naturally, we were worried about what would happen to Kevin. About an hour later, he rejoined us and I could tell he'd been crying and was very distressed. I didn't think the Customs men had touched him physically but it seemed obvious that he had been threatened and intimidated.

The feeling among the players was that we wanted to go home. I certainly wasn't in the right frame of mind to play the game because of what they'd done to Kevin. He'd done nothing wrong. The Yugoslavian authorities wanted to quickly sweep the incident under the carpet and tried to pretend it had never happened. The Football Association officials who were travelling with us told us it would be best if we continued with the tour.

I have since spoken to Kevin about the incident and he told me that they had mistaken him for a supporter. Kevin says he was taken into the Customs offices, where he was quite badly beaten. I'd never realised the extent of his mistreatment because he'd been too upset to tell us all the details at the time.

The FA Secretary, Ted Croker, lodged a complaint with the Yugoslavians but we were persuaded to carry on with the game because of the political unrest that had existed in the country. We drew the match 2–2. Kevin Keegan scored one of our goals, which seemed the perfect ending to his, and our, troubled trip to Yugoslavia.

CHAPTER TWELVE
Superstar

During my career, I didn't do many things apart from play football and enjoy my family life but during the summer of 1974 I was persuaded to appear on a television programme called *Superstars*. The idea was that top sportsmen from different disciplines competed against each other to discover who the overall superstar was.

The list of those who took part was truly impressive, with footballers like Kevin Keegan and Mike Channon competing against Formula One driver Nicky Lauda, shot-putter Geoff Capes and boxer John Conteh. There's a new version of *Superstars* on TV now but the competitors don't include top football stars. You couldn't include them in the show these days.

Can you imagine sportsmen with high profiles like Michael Schumacher, Steven Gerrard and Frank Lampard taking part today? Lloyds of London wouldn't be prepared to provide the insurance cover and, of course, the football clubs and agents simply wouldn't allow their clients to participate.

I agreed to take part because I loved a sporting challenge and

I'd always been curious about my general levels of fitness. The thought of competing against people from other sports appealed to me. The competition consisted of a series of heats using various different sports.

I enjoy any types of games or competition: tennis, running, cycling, gymnasium work, that sort of thing. One of the events I won was pistol shooting and we even played some cricket in one of the heats.

I wasn't allowed to take part in anything that resembled football, so I couldn't do the penalty taking. We had to choose two events to leave out, so, as well as the penalty taking, I took the chance to avoid the swimming, which I was never particularly good at. I was at the peak of my fitness at that time, mainly thanks to the years of working with Malcolm Allison.

I competed in *Superstars* twice: in the summer of 1974 and the following year, too. In one of them, staged at the Crystal Palace athletics stadium, I was up against the Olympic hurdling gold medallist David Hemery, who'd smashed the world record over 400 metres in the 1968 Mexico Olympic Games. The race took place over four laps, which is about one mile. I think he had to start a lap behind the rest of us.

Hemery was allowed to take part because he'd already dropped out of two other running events. We were to race over a steeplechase course, with the water jump included. I'd never hurdled before but soon got used to it. It was a bit like jumping over the tackle of a defender.

I was desperate to do well in the race and I was keen to measure myself against an Olympic champion. I won by more than a lap, which meant if he'd started level with me I'd still have beaten him. Maybe I kidded myself that day – after all, it wasn't the same as winning an Olympic gold and, to be honest, he slipped and fell at the water jump, which cost him a few yards. I certainly finished well in front of everybody else, though. Running four laps was right up my street.

Malcolm Macdonald took part in the 100 metres. No one stood a chance. I was still coming out of the blocks as he crossed the finishing line; in fact, by the time I crossed the line he'd got changed and made a cup of tea!

Malcolm was a player I admired. I remember him being marked by Tommy Booth in one game at Maine Road. Malcolm was in the old inside-left position, on the Kippax side of the ground. The ball was knocked over the top into our half and while Tommy was still thinking about turning, Macdonald had already gone ten yards.

A similar incident happened a few minutes later but this time Tommy was ready for him and was standing ten yards inside him instead of being tight up against him. Malcolm Macdonald was a good striker – a bit on the greedy side, as all good strikers are – but he had real pace and was very strong.

I didn't train specifically for *Superstars*, though I noticed that one or two of the others seemed to take it more seriously than the rest. John Conteh had practised cycling, weightlifting and sit-ups. I just turned up and got on with it. There were times, though, when some extra training would have helped me avoid embarrassment.

Although I enjoyed cycling, I hadn't prepared myself for riding at top speed, around a corner, on a flat athletics track. Mike Channon and I competed against each other in one race, with Marie and Mike's wife sitting at the first bend to get the best possible view.

Once the starting gun was fired, we cycled as fast as we could without really thinking about how we would keep on the bike as we turned hard into the corner. Mike just went straight on and ended up heading for our wives, who had to dive out of the way for fear of being hit. He was in hysterics.

Unlike me, Mike took part in the swimming. I don't know which two events he dropped out of but he must have thought he was *really* bad at the others if he chose to stay in the swimming! Marie and I went to watch and sat on the spectator terracing down the side of the pool.

The race wasn't at all like the Olympic events we're used to seeing on the TV, where the gap between first and last can be measured in tenths of a second. The leader could be half a length ahead, although Mike was probably even further back than that. He wasn't just finding it difficult to keep up with the others, he was struggling to keep his head above the water.

As Marie and I enjoyed the fun, we slowly realised that Mike was going up and down in the middle of the pool, with bubbles everywhere and his arms flailing all over the place. Eventually, he managed to doggy paddle to the side but the truth is he nearly drowned.

I loved taking part in *Superstars* but unfortunately I didn't win either of the overall competitions. I finished third in one but the sweetest moment for me was definitely beating David Hemery on the track.

The previous football season had been unsettling for me, with Johnny Hart, Ron Saunders and Tony Book all taking their turn as manager along with the change of chairman. Although we'd reached the League Cup final, it had been my unhappiest year at the club, so I was more determined than ever that the new season would be a good one when we came together for pre-season training in the summer of 1974.

As usual, there were comings and goings among the players, with the biggest surprise being the sale of Francis Lee to Derby County. Not only had that 1–0 win at Old Trafford proved to be the last club game for Denis Law, it was Franny's final game for City, too. Among the new faces brought in was midfield player Asa Hartford.

Booky was starting to make his mark, though some supporters suggested it was Peter Swales who had decided to sell Francis Lee. A vociferous group of fans thought Francis had been involved in bringing down Ron Saunders. I think Booky had simply decided Franny's best days were behind him. I felt Franny still had a lot to offer and I was disappointed that he was moving away.

In those days, players tended to spend longer at one club than they do now and I always imagined that we'd all stay at City until our playing days were over. I think it was a mistake to sell Francis Lee but I think he was far more disappointed than me; indeed, I think he was quite angry by the way the whole thing was handled.

Despite the changes, the new season started well enough and I was enjoying my football. Our side was full of attacking flair and we scored plenty of goals in the opening games, starting with a 4–0 win against West Ham United. By the middle of November, we were at the top of the table and I believed we could repeat our title success of 1968.

We'd beaten Liverpool 2–0 at Maine Road, thanks to goals from Dennis Tueart and Rodney Marsh, and we were 2–1 winners against the champions, Leeds United. Dennis had a similar approach to the game as Francis Lee – direct and aggressive – and he was a regular goal scorer.

Only two or three points separated the teams in the top half of the division as we approached Christmas. Our holiday fixtures were against two of our closest rivals, Liverpool at Anfield on Boxing Day, and Derby County at Maine Road two days later.

Things started badly with a 1–4 defeat on Merseyside but we were confident we'd bounce back against Derby, where we'd be reunited with our old friend Francis Lee. Naturally, the crowd gave Franny a great reception, which he fully deserved. Many of the supporters shared my view that the club had sold him too early. It was certainly nice to see him again but of course we were all determined to show him that City were top dogs.

At half-time, we were 0–1 down, thanks to a great shot from Henry Newton. We started the second half well and eventually Dennis Tueart set me up for the equaliser. It was to be Franny's day, though, and with about 15 minutes left, he drove a shot past Joe Corrigan into the top corner and we lost the game 1–2. He'd proved his point and I've never seen him grin as broadly as he did when he scored that day.

Derby County went on to win the League Championship that season and I've wondered many times since then whether we would have won the title if Franny had still been with us. Later that season, Derby beat us again at the Baseball Ground.

We went out of the League Cup at Old Trafford, Second Division United beating us 0–1 with a Gerry Daly penalty. That was a major disappointment. Losing to United was never something I enjoyed but thankfully I was only on the losing side in five of the twenty-one derbies I played in.

The FA Cup proved to be equally frustrating, with us going out in the third round, losing 0–2 to Newcastle United at Maine Road. The game should have been played at St James's Park but the FA had switched the venue because Newcastle had experienced crowd trouble at a previous match.

Another new City player had arrived by then, with centre-forward Joe Royle joining us from Everton. I knew Joe from the England team and knew how good he was. I had no doubts that he would add extra quality to our team. Our home form was excellent but we seemed to struggle away from Maine Road.

I felt I was playing as well as ever but because of the turnover of players I constantly had to adapt to the way the others timed their runs. In front of the Maine Road faithful, we always turned on the style, playing fast-flowing, entertaining football and generally scoring plenty of goals.

One of the most disappointing games of that season, from my point of view, was the game at Leicester on 8 March 1975. I'd always enjoyed playing as a goalkeeper as a kid and occasionally in training. I'd played so well in goal for a while as a 15 year old for Stockton and Billingham Technical College that my teacher had recommended me as a keeper to a scout from Sheffield Wednesday. I knew I was more likely to further my career as an inside-right, so I rejected the opportunity. Although I knew I was quite good as a goalkeeper, I just saw it as a bit of fun in the midweek games and a chance to play in a different position after two games at the weekend as a midfielder.

One of my ambitions, therefore, was to play in goal for City. I was the nominated stand-by goalkeeper in case of injury during a game. I thought my long-awaited chance had come at Filbert Street when Keith MacRae was taken off early in the game with an injury. I was running through the centre-circle at the time of the incident and by the time I'd run back to our penalty area Mike Doyle had already put the goalkeeper's shirt on.

'What's going on?' I asked Doyley. 'You just concentrate on doing what you do and I'll stop them scoring,' he shouted and I had no choice but to carry on as normal.

After the game, he argued that it made more sense for Alan Oakes to drop back into defence to cover *his* position than it did to shuffle things around throughout the team to allow me to take over in goal. I couldn't agree at the time – I just wanted to play in goal.

The score was 0–0 when Doyley took over from MacRae and he kept Leicester out until the closing few moments, when Bob Lee scored the winner to leave everyone deflated.

I can still remember some of the saves I made during my time in goal at Billingham – particularly that one from the chip over my head that I mentioned in Chapter One! I reckon I could have done a decent job as a goalkeeper and although I enjoyed every minute of my career in football, I still wish I could have shown the City fans how good I might have been in goal.

That match also proved to be Glyn Pardoe's last in the first team, though he continued his fight for full fitness in the reserves for another season and a half.

Just three matches later, it was the turn of Mike Summerbee to move on. He left us just ahead of the transfer deadline to join Burnley and within the space of a few months three of the most influential players of our era had gone. Although I've always taken life as it comes and simply got on with my job, I was sad to see such great players and good friends leave.

We finished that campaign in eighth place, which sounds worse than it was. We'd had a very good season in the league and had played some wonderful football at times. Despite all the changes that were occurring in the team, I don't think I'd ever played any better.

One of my favourite goals came in a match towards the end of that season. It was in a home game against Burnley when Dennis Tueart played a square ball to me 25 to 30 yards out from goal. I hit it perfectly with the outside of my right foot, aiming the ball three or four feet to the left-hand side of the goal. The swerve brought it in, just enough to nestle perfectly into the top corner, just beyond goalkeeper Alan Stevenson's reach.

The only goal I scored that was better was at White Hart Lane. That day I'd received the ball down the left wing. As I checked my stride, I clipped it over the defender near the corner flag. As I let the ball bounce once, I checked where the Spurs goalkeeper, Pat Jennings, was positioned. He's one of the best goalkeepers I've ever faced. It wasn't the best of angles but I caught it about two feet off the ground with my toe bent as far as it would go to get maximum top spin on the ball. I hit it so it would dip over Jennings into the goal.

Alan Ball had been a spectator at that game and during a recent conversation he told me he had always believed it to be a fluke. I assured him that it had been nothing of the sort. I knew exactly what I was trying to do and I believe that it was the best goal I ever scored.

The former Leeds United manager Don Revie had taken charge of England by now. He had a different approach from both Alf Ramsey and Joe Mercer.

It might seem trivial but under Revie we changed kit suppliers to Admiral and I found their shirts uncomfortable. It was like wearing a shirt made from cardboard. One of his new ideas was to get us to play bingo before games, telling us it was a way to relax and take our minds off the match. I didn't enjoy it at all. It certainly wasn't part of my normal build-up routine.

There was never a deliberate movement against Revie by the players, but he wasn't as popular as Alf had been. I also think he suffered from being the manager who had to follow in the footsteps of the man who'd guided England to success in the 1966 World Cup. Don Revie never lived up to his own expectations as England manager, which was a shame.

As usual, I enjoyed the home internationals against Scotland, Wales and Northern Ireland. The game against Scotland at Wembley proved to be highly significant – but for all the wrong reasons.

We won the game 5–1, which was particularly pleasing, but

I've seen lots of photographs since of the thousands of Scots fans who invaded the pitch, swinging on the cross bars and causing havoc after the match had ended.

As with the derby at Old Trafford in 1974, we hadn't really been fully aware of what was going on until we were safely in the dressing-room. I was certainly aware of the need to leave the pitch quickly at the end of the game. I've previously described the atmosphere at England versus Scotland games as electric. Sadly, that day it was spoilt and the home internationals were cancelled as a result, which I believe has been a terrible loss to our domestic football programme.

That was the end of another football season, so for a few months I was able to spend a bit more time with the family. Despite now being a married man, my interest in horse racing had continued and I was still popping into the Bell Waldron restaurant in Whitefield whenever I could.

After selling both Stay Back and Stay Bell, the third horse I was part owner of was Baker Brown, named after Tony Brown, the local baker who was part of our little consortium. Marie and I enjoyed our days out watching it run at the races.

Watching it run; that's a joke!

Standing in the winner's enclosure at Beverley when the horse had finished third was a particularly proud moment. Tony Murray had been the jockey and he was disappointed. He told me that if he'd known the horse better he would have won that day. It didn't matter to me – I was just happy that the horse had been placed.

The summer of 1975 promised to be one of the most exciting of my life because Marie was pregnant again. She'd lost two babies previously, so it was also an anxious time for us. We spent some time living with Marie's parents, as she wasn't feeling very well. I tried to do as much as I could to make life easier for her but, of course, during most of the pregnancy I was still training and playing every day.

Once the season was over I could put all my energy into being there by Marie's side. Eventually, on 4 July 1975, our little girl was born, prematurely, in hospital. I was at Marie's side all the way, doing as much as I could to help her through it all.

We called our baby Dawn. Marie's mother and father had recently returned from a holiday in Barbados and had met a girl called Dawn who they'd clearly been impressed by. I fell in love with the name, although Marie's choice had been Alexandria. We ganged up on her and persuaded her that we should call the baby Dawn Alexandria.

Having a child changes your life, as any parent will tell you, and we were no exception. I've never been as proud in my life.

I was already committed to making my second appearance on *Superstars*, in Aldershot, so having been with Marie throughout the crucial moments we decided I should still go and take part. The day after Dawn's birth I went off to compete but my life would never be the same again and I wouldn't have wanted it any other way.

CHAPTER THIRTEEN
Just When It Was Going So Well

As I returned to pre-season training in the summer of 1975, I felt as optimistic as ever. I was twenty-nine years old and I reckoned I had another five or six years ahead of me as a professional footballer. I felt that I was playing as well as at any time in my career. I still had the athleticism that had been my trademark but now had years of experience, too, plus I'd continued to learn the game, as all good players do.

Our big summer signing was the England centre-half Dave Watson, who came from Sunderland for £200,000. Despite the loss of Lee, Summerbee, Young and Pardoe from our championship-winning side, we had brought in Rodney Marsh, Joe Royle, Dave Watson, Asa Hartford and Dennis Tueart, so there was every reason to believe another title or cup win was just around the corner.

We started the season with an emphatic 3–0 win against Norwich at Maine Road, with Dennis Tueart getting two goals and me scoring the other. I couldn't understand what went wrong in the next three games because after a 1–1 draw at home to Leicester we lost two away games in a row, at Coventry and Aston Villa.

There was a definite pattern emerging at the start of that season with comfortable home wins, including two 4–0s against Newcastle and Middlesbrough, and narrow away defeats. I wasn't particularly worried by the sequence at that stage and assumed that once the new players had settled in we would climb into the top three.

One of the things I was looking forward to most was the resumption of the league derbies with United, who were now back in the First Division. The first meeting was at Maine Road in September. Joe Royle pressured Jimmy Nicholl into a spectacular own goal, before David McCreery put them level.

Mike Doyle crossed for Joe to make it 2–1 but Lou Macari's immediate reply proved to be the final goal. All four goals were scored within ten frantic first-half minutes. Alan Oakes had a late chance to win the game for us with a header but we had to settle for a 2–2 draw.

We bounced back in our next game by winning 3–2 at Arsenal, so when we were drawn against United in the fourth round of the League Cup we relished the chance to make sure we beat them this time. We'd reached that stage of the competition by knocking out Norwich City after two replays, settled by a 6–1 win on neutral territory at Chelsea's Stamford Bridge, and then a 2–1 victory against Nottingham Forest.

My England career was going from strength to strength at this time and after initially feeling in awe of the 1966 World Cup winners when I'd first joined the squad, I now felt relaxed, as I did with City. I felt I was performing as well as ever at international level.

One of my best performances had been against Czechoslovakia in October 1974, when I'd scored twice in a 3–0 win at Wembley. Almost exactly a year later, with the visit of United just a fortnight away, I travelled to Bratislava with England for a European Championship qualifier, which we lost 1–2. That proved to be the last of my 48 England appearances, though as we flew back to the UK I had no idea that I would never reach my half-century of appearances for my country.

Back with City, we'd had some disappointing results in away games but rarely failed to play well, and win, at home. The match before the visit of United in the cup was typical. We beat Birmingham City 2–0 and I scored both goals. That game had seemed so easy to me. If I hit a 30-yard cross-field ball to Dennis Tueart on one wing or to young Peter Barnes on the other, it just 'pinged' wherever I meant it to go, right to their feet.

Naturally, having played well in the game four days earlier, I couldn't wait to play against United. If we won the game, as I felt sure we would, we'd be through to the quarter-finals. Everything seemed to be going better than I could have wished.

Wednesday, 12 November 1975 was the date of that League Cup derby against United; it was to be a date I would never forget. We were determined to beat them, as we knew we should have been victorious when we'd played them in the league game a month earlier. Their confidence had returned after a year in Division Two but we believed it would be our day.

I always enjoyed playing under floodlights and there was a tremendous atmosphere as we ran out and prepared to get under way. Within a minute, we were ahead, with Dennis Tueart scoring the goal. United were rattled. As we pressed forward for a second goal, I received a pass through the centre-circle from Dennis.

I was in the old-fashioned inside-right position as I made my way towards United's goal at the Platt Lane end of the ground. I'd run about ten or fifteen yards into space, as things opened up for me because the United players had been drawn towards Dennis. I had a bit of space in front of me and I was preparing to shoot.

Paddy Roche was in goal and the pitch was a bit bobbly, as many surfaces were at that time of year. In the back of my mind, I was thinking that I might have a shot, as Paddy wasn't the best of goalkeepers. At that stage, I didn't really feel I had much of a choice, apart from having a crack at goal. Out of the corner of my eye, I saw a player coming across in front of me and I decided I had three options. I picked the wrong one.

The first option was to take a shot, if the ball sat up in the right position. The second was to increase my forward pace and try to go away from the player. The third choice was to stop, drag the ball back, let him go across me and then I'd go on clear, towards goal. I selected the last one.

I dragged it back, which left me balanced on my right leg, with all six studs in the ground. I could now see that it was Martin Buchan who was challenging me. His tackle smacked me just below the knee, on the right leg, which had my full weight on it.

It felt like my leg had been screwed into the ground. My knee bent backwards, bursting blood vessels in the bottom of my thigh and in the top of my calf. All the ligaments in my knee were torn. Within seconds, the knee was just a bag of blood. I knew straight away that it was a bad injury.

It wasn't the pain that bothered me the most as I was being carried off by our physiotherapist Freddie Griffiths and his assistant Roy Bailey, it was fearing how bad the injury was. I shouted up to Freddie, 'They've friggin' hurt me, Fred.' Within 30 seconds, my knee had swollen to the size of a football.

Very soon, I was in an ambulance on the way to hospital, where I was to stay for several days. My leg was black and blue from the hip joint right down to my ankle. I was quite generally unwell too, not just from the injury but also the shock to my system. I was told by the doctors that the trauma was similar to that suffered by someone involved in a serious car crash.

Freddie Griffiths told me a couple of days later that there had been a definite risk of thrombosis, which could have killed me. I hate to imagine the complications that might have set in if the coin had flipped down on the other side. I reckon I was quite lucky in the end. I never considered it at the time but I guess they might have had to amputate the leg. As far as I was concerned, there was only one thought in my mind: that I'd get the best possible attention and make a compete recovery.

As usual, Marie hadn't been at the game, but she'd been listening on the radio and she says the impression she got was that the injury wasn't that bad. I'd suffered plenty of injuries during my career, so it wasn't anything new for Marie. A few minutes later, she received a call from the club telling her that I'd been taken to hospital. It's hard to imagine it now but in those days the hospital authorities discouraged even close family from visiting a patient out of hours, so she was advised to stay at home and visit me the next day.

The newspapers the following day suggested that I might be out of action for about four weeks, although I knew things were more serious than that. The knee was a mess. As well as ligament and muscle damage, the cartilages had been destroyed and, of course, there'd been massive internal bleeding.

Perhaps with today's surgical techniques my treatment would have been different, but that kind of expertise simply didn't exist at the time. The first operation I had was to remove the congealed blood. After surgery, they immobilised my leg, which with hindsight was probably a mistake.

I believe that if I'd kept bending the leg and been able to

mobilise at an earlier stage, it would have helped the healing process. To have it in a straight-legged position meant everything just congealed even more inside the knee. It was as if the joint had been super-glued. When the plaster was eventually removed, I couldn't even bend my knee.

I don't blame Martin Buchan for the injury. I know that there are players in the game who set out to kick you and injure you if they can but I don't think he was that type of player. I was a little disappointed, though, that he didn't visit me during my time in hospital. If it had been me who'd done that to him, I'd have gone to see him, as long as I knew in my own mind that I hadn't done it on purpose.

He didn't come to see me and only he can tell you what was going on in his mind at that time. I've always maintained the challenge was an accident but he's never apologised to me.

Ian Cheeseman, who's worked with me on this book, rang Martin Buchan to ask for his version of events and I'm told he didn't want to make any comment. However, he did tell Ian, 'I have never had any problems sleeping at night over that tackle. The injury was caused by the fact that his studs were in the ground at the time of impact. The referee never even stopped the game, so the tackle couldn't have been that bad.'

Martin's comments don't change my views and as far as I'm concerned there are more important things to worry about.

There have been a few serious injuries in derby matches; I guess it's because of the extra 'edge' in those games. I'd been stretchered off at Old Trafford in March 1968, a game we'd won 3–1. Francis Burns brought me down from behind to give away a penalty, which Franny Lee scored to complete the win. That time I hadn't been caught on my standing leg, so the injury hadn't been as bad, though I did spend a week or two in plaster that went halfway up my leg!

Glyn Pardoe and United's John Aston and Tony Dunne all suffered injuries in derbies and, more recently, Alfie Haaland, of course. Is it coincidence? Glyn's injury was bad, too. He nearly lost his leg as a result of his problems but he'd battled back to play again and his determination was something I knew I could match.

Naturally, my initial recuperation was at home and one of the best things about the situation I found myself in was that I spent a lot of time with our baby daughter, Dawn. I couldn't crawl about on the floor, of course, but she'd sit on my good knee for hours, while I watched the TV.

I spent most of my time with my ankle resting on some pillows, so that it was higher than my knee. The idea was that the fluid in the joint would drain back into my body from that position. Every time I dropped my ankle lower than the height of my groin I suffered violent 'pins and needles' in my leg. When I had to stand to go to the toilet or go to another room, I experienced tremendous pain.

I felt great relief when I was able to walk again a few weeks later. After all the things I'd been through, I was grateful for that. I'm a very single-minded person, so as soon as I was back on my feet I wanted to start training again, planning my comeback. I tried to put the memories of the terrible damage done to my leg to the back of my mind and thought only about getting back into the first team.

Within a few days of being back on my feet, I was trying to run a little and felt that if I could play a few reserve games I'd soon be back to normal. I wasn't thinking rationally; I was just being me: single-minded and stubborn. I blocked out the discomfort, ignored the fact I couldn't fully bend the knee and just got on with it. My first game back was on Saturday, 17 January, just over two months after being rushed to hospital. It was a reserve game at Blackpool.

Ironically, Glyn Pardoe, who was still battling to get back to full fitness after his terrible injury in a derby, also played in that match, which we drew 0–0 in front of a crowd of just 582. I soon realised that I was out of my depth. My head was telling me to chase a ball out to the corner flag and my legs just wouldn't take me there. I felt embarrassed by my poor contribution to the team and felt I was letting down the other players, who included Gary Owen, Roger Palmer and Tony Henry. The following day I asked Booky not to play me again in the reserves for a while.

I concentrated all my efforts on getting the knee stronger and I hoped I might be ready in time to play in the League Cup final on 28 February, which the lads had qualified for by beating Middlesbrough 4–0 at Maine Road.

I soon realised I wouldn't make it and that I would have to settle for being a spectator. Marie also went to the game. She'd only seen me play once, in the League Cup final two years earlier against Wolves, and in truth she only went to the 1976 game because the players' wives had organised another shopping trip.

Having beaten Mansfield and Middlesbrough to earn their trip to the final, we were favourites to beat Newcastle, who'd been affected by a flu bug. Their strikers were Malcolm Macdonald and Alan Gowling, so they certainly would be no pushovers. Peter Barnes scored the first goal, with Gowling equalising just before half-time. Dennis Tueart's famous overhead kick, just after the break, proved to be the winner.

It was agony watching the rest of the lads playing that day. I wasn't a good spectator. By the time they'd received the trophy and done their lap of honour, I'd made my way down to the dressing-room and congratulated them all as they came back in.

The following day, we had an open-topped bus tour around Manchester that ended with a civic reception at the town hall. I didn't really feel that I belonged there, as I'd not played in the final, but our magnificent supporters chanted my name until I was persuaded to go on to the balcony with the rest of the players to take a bow. It was a special moment for me to know that I hadn't been forgotten.

Back at home, I was more determined than ever to return to full fitness and play as soon as possible but the reality was that I had no idea when I would be back. I'm a very independent person who doesn't like asking people for favours and at times I felt helpless. Marie was like my nurse. I had to shout her whenever I needed anything and despite her own busy lifestyle she was always there in a flash.

Dave Watson and his wife, Penny, used to visit me a lot. Dave was a great babysitter as well as being a great player. At my worst times, Big Joe Corrigan had carried me down the stairs and was one of those who'd take me to Maine Road.

Soon after that trip to Wembley, I felt I wanted to try another game in the reserves. I played in a match at Everton and although I still knew I wasn't right, I was determined to continue, believing I could run through the discomfort and that eventually I'd be back to normal. Nearly 2,000 supporters came to the game against Leeds United at Maine Road on 10 March, my first home game since the injury. Their support gave me a tremendous lift.

After two more reserve games, I made my first-team comeback in a home match against Derby County at Maine Road on 10 April 1976. I hadn't played at the top level for six months and I was relieved that I could finally put all the frustration behind me. The crowd that day was over 42,000 – nearly 10,000 more than normal – and again I was told that many of the extra supporters had come to the game to see my return.

Things seemed to go quite well. I wasn't as mobile as I had been before the injury but I felt confident I would get stronger. It was an eventful match to be involved in, with seven goals. We won 4–3. The following day, I could feel a reaction in my knee, so I quickly realised I'd have to miss the midweek trip to Newcastle but I returned the following Saturday at Leeds. I scored our consolation goal in a 1–2 defeat, from the edge of their box.

I was encouraged by the football I'd played and I remained optimistic that, with a few months to work more on the strength in my knee and my overall fitness, I'd be back to my best by the start of the following season. Before that, there were three more games to go, starting with the visit of Liverpool, which proved a big disappointment: we lost 0–3.

Booky asked me to play at right-back in the next game, a home match against Arsenal. The idea was to get me involved in some tackling, which Tony thought would build up my confidence in the strength of my knee. Among the players I faced that day were Liam Brady, Trevor Ross and Alex Cropley.

As we defended the North Stand, I was playing in front of the dugouts and Ross tried to go past me. I challenged him, just as I would have done at my peak level of fitness, and as the tackle was completed I felt something pop out of the side of my knee. I knew instinctively that this was not good.

It was another major setback and I didn't play in the last game of the season at Old Trafford. Little did I know how significant this second injury to the knee would prove to be. In hindsight, I know I came back too early and perhaps if I'd waited until the following season, I might have built up enough strength in my knee to have prevented further harm to the joint.

CHAPTER FOURTEEN
Never Giving In

The summer of 1976 was one of the hottest I can remember. We had weeks of unbroken sunshine and the temperatures were much higher than normal. For the tennis players at Wimbledon and the visiting West Indian cricketers it must have seemed perfect but there was to be no summer break for me. My only goal was to spend every minute I could recovering from this latest setback.

I used to go to the ground every morning at nine o'clock. Assistant physio Roy Bailey went miles out of his way to give me a lift to Maine Road. I'd work until lunchtime before taking a break for lunch. I'd then carry on until about six o'clock, when Roy would take me home again.

I'd run up and down the steps at the back of the Kippax Stand trying to get more flexibility in the knee and Freddie would go running with me around the streets of Moss Side. I tried everything – weights, Jacuzzis, stretching, hot baths – the lot. By the start of the new season, ever the optimist, I felt like I'd be back playing soon.

When the new season started in mid-August, I was still battling to get the flexibility back in the knee but remained confident that if I worked hard enough, whatever had popped out of my knee in the game against Arsenal would eventually click back into place and I'd be back playing again.

I found it increasingly difficult to adjust to a routine that didn't include a match at the weekend. I was used to building up to the climax of a game on a Saturday. Now Saturdays had lost their significance and at times I honestly didn't know what day of the week it was.

I didn't spend any time training with the rest of the first-team players, I was usually there at different times to them and I started to lose contact with what was going on or how the first team were playing. I didn't go to the games: I couldn't stand watching, knowing I couldn't be part of it.

Now and again, I'd get an update from one of the other injured players. Peter Barnes spent a few days next to me on the treatment table and he remembers some of the things that happened to me. He told me, 'Freddie used to work on improving flexibility in your knee. The noises and cracking sounds that were made during those sessions made my stomach turn.'

Although I always felt my return was just a few weeks away, my knee wasn't improving as dramatically as I'd hoped. By November, I was advised that another operation might be the solution. Previously, I'd had the internal cartilage removed, which had broken into small pieces as a result of the injury.

It was now decided that the structure I'd felt pop out of my knee had to be dealt with. It felt like there was something, possibly congealed blood, sandwiched between the layers of muscle on the inside of my knee.

I was aware that people were starting to suggest I'd never play again but, rather than letting those comments have a negative effect, it made me even more determined to make a complete recovery. When Tony Book visited me in hospital after the operation, I told him I'd be back soon. I certainly got used to hospital food after many stays for operations or manipulative treatment!

All I thought about day and night was getting fit again, so I was pleasantly surprised and very encouraged when I received a phone call from the England manager, Don Revie. He told me that I was still very much part of his plans for the World Cup in Argentina in 1978. He asked me to meet him at Maine Road before a game against West Ham, where he told me that once I was fit again there would be a place for me in the England side.

My attitude was simple: if there was to be another snag, I'd just battle on and overcome it – I would be back. I used to set targets for my return but I didn't make them public. At home, Marie did everything she could to support me and as soon as I walked through the door our baby daughter Dawn would lift my spirits.

The TV programme *Nationwide* did a feature on me and I received lots of letters and cards, which helped. The fans were terrific but those long football-less days were the blackest moments of my life.

At some points, it seemed like time had stopped. Every week, it was the same routine, with no end in sight. I felt like I knew every step on the Kippax terracing and every flagstone on the streets around Moss Side.

It never occurred to me that there could be other treatments for my injury. That was for other people to consider. I simply concentrated on doing whatever they told me and on getting fit as quickly as I could to help the recovery.

Eventually, in March 1977, 11 months after that last first-team game against Arsenal, I was as ready as I might ever be to try to play again. My return to action was unannounced and came in front of just 322 fans against Sheffield United Reserves at Maine Road.

I have to admit I was far more hesitant in the tackle this time. After all, I'd come through a lot to get to this stage and I didn't want to be back at square one again. Among those in the City reserve team that day was Paul Power.

Tony Book explained the circumstances of my return in his programme notes a few days later:

> One of the most satisfying selections made at Maine Road this year was the return to action last week of Colin Bell, who has had an agonising period of inactivity since that crippling injury he received against Manchester United in November 1975.
>
> I brought Colin back into harness against Sheffield United Reserves last mid-week and I did it without advance notification. Colin has been under a lot of pressure to state a comeback date. He has been aware of the whispers that have suggested he would have to pack up the game and I did not think it advisable to announce his return publicly, thus subjecting him to searching scrutiny when his real need is to be gently re-introduced to regular games.
>
> His programme now consists of a series of rehabilitating games with the reserves and I am hoping that his strength and confidence will grow with each appearance and that those well-known classical touches will soon be in evidence.
>
> We don't expect too much too soon – nor should any of the fans. I don't want him to go flat out at this stage –

there is no point in taking risks. We have sorely missed him for a long time, and to be absolutely certain that we have him back at his very best we would be foolish not to be prepared to wait just a little longer. The day he pulls on a first-team shirt again will be my finest tonic for many a long day.

With those thoughts in mind, I played in nine more reserve games that season, scoring at Preston and against Derby County. The first team seemed unaffected by my absence and had a great season, finishing second in the league, just behind Liverpool. The City chairman, Peter Swales, summed up the campaign in his end-of-season notes in the match programme by saying, 'Nobody's going to tell me that we wouldn't have won the League Championship if we'd had Colin available. Belly is the greatest player I've ever seen, and I include George Best.'

Despite another summer of endless fitness work and ever-more imaginative ways of trying to get back the full flexibility into my knee, I started the 1977–78 season playing in the reserves and still unsure as to when I'd be ready for the first team. By 17 December, I'd played 17 games in the Central League and we were up near the top of the table.

As well as getting as fit as I could during my long absence, I'd got used to running with a limp and had adapted to playing without the bursts of acceleration I'd been used to. I still had plenty of stamina but couldn't turn as quickly.

More than two years since I'd suffered the injury, and countless operations later, I was named as a first-team substitute against Newcastle United on Boxing Day 1977. Tony Book told me he'd probably bring me on in the second half for the last 20 minutes, feeling it would be too much for me to play the full 90 minutes.

I warmed up a couple of times during that first 45 minutes and each time I got off the bench the supporters gave me a fantastic round of applause. The players came in at half-time with the score at 0–0 and Paul Power reported an injury. 'Colin, I'm bringing you on for Paul at the start of the second half,' Booky told me, 'so get yourself ready.'

Within seconds, word had spread to the supporters and by the time I followed the team up the tunnel to come on as substitute there were fans hanging over the side shouting encouragement to me. The second I came into view, the crowd rose to their feet and made more noise than I've ever heard in my life.

I'm not an emotional person but I got a big lump in my throat. It felt like their ovation, for *me*, went on for ever; I'm told it was about four minutes before they stopped. Those moments were better than winning all the trophies I had, because it was the supporters thanking me for all that I'd done for them. I knew it was for me personally. A few people, grown men, have actually told me they cried, which shows how much it meant to them.

The supporters sang songs for me throughout my career and I've never known another player to get such great backing. They were always on my side and knew that I'd always given them 100 per cent of my effort in return. That game against Newcastle was the highlight of my career; it's a shame it worked out that way.

The atmosphere throughout the second half was as electric as it gets. Unless you were there, you can't imagine what it was like – you'd have heard a pin drop in the first half but wouldn't have heard a plane crash in the second.

I can't even remember touching the ball in that game and at times I felt like things were passing me by but suddenly we were 4–0 up, which was all down to the crowd. The supporters must have terrified Newcastle United. I didn't feel any pain in the knee that day – I felt like I was floating on air.

My teammate Tommy Booth, who also played, once said in an interview that he'll never forget that day either: 'I've played in cup finals and before crowds of 100,000 but I've never heard a roar like the one they gave for Colin's return. It was unbelievable. It was something special to be there that day and see that sort of reaction from the crowd. Colin was a world-class player and we all just wanted to see him play again.'

Paul Power, the player I'd replaced at half-time, also said: 'Colin Bell is a legend to me. I've been a City fan all my life. I wasn't sure if the City fans were cheering so much because I'd gone off or because he was coming on! Joking apart, I would rather have been substituted that day by Colin than anyone else.'

Humbling words indeed from two good friends.

I was back, although I knew things still weren't right. However, I believed that playing at first-team pace would soon get me back to the way I'd been before the injury and I was getting tremendous support from everyone at City. I started the next game away to Middlesbrough and stayed in the side as we went on a run of seven successive league wins. I played in 16 consecutive league and cup games and scored a couple of goals.

To those looking in from the outside, it might have seemed things were going well for me but I knew I was still limping and was nowhere near my best. We struggled in March, losing at Arsenal and then drawing at United and Wolves. After another draw, this time at home to Middlesbrough, Tony Book suggested I have another try in the reserves and left me out of the first team for the next game against Newcastle United.

I was familiar with the reserve side, having played so many games for them during my recuperation, so I slotted back in quickly. We were on the verge of winning the Central League

Championship and I played a further five games with them to help secure the title.

We were presented with the trophy after a 1–0 win against Liverpool in front of over 4,000 supporters at Maine Road. Our team that day was: MacRae, Ranson, Sherlock, Coughlin, Evans, Power, Keegan, Bell, Palmer, Henry and Henderson.

It was the first time the reserves had won their league. I consider my part in that success to be one of my proudest achievements. The presentation was at the Bowdon Hotel in Altrincham. The reserve-team coach, Dave Ewing, took us all down and I treasure the medal I received that day as much as anything I own. I'm proud to have been involved in another big part of the club's history.

I played four more games in the first team at the end of the season and we finished fourth. My biggest disappointment had been losing to Arsenal in the fifth round of the League Cup. I thought we would win it that season but we lost the replay at Highbury, 0–1, to go out of the competition.

Although I remained hopeful that my knee would suddenly click back into place and I'd have the full movement again, I knew I couldn't have gone to Argentina with England that summer, even if they'd qualified. I had to settle for watching some of the games on TV. The 1978 World Cup finals should have been *my* finals, coming at my peak, but it wasn't to be.

There were plenty of new faces in the City side by now. Mike Doyle had gone to Stoke City, Dennis Tueart had left for New York Cosmos and Joe Royle had moved on to Bristol City. The new players were less familiar to me but it was hoped the likes of Colin Viljoen, the Futcher brothers, Paul and Ron, Mike Channon and the Polish international Kaziu Deyna would help us overtake United as the bigger club in Manchester. Certainly, that was the hope of chairman Peter Swales.

My only concern was to prove to myself that I could still play like I'd done in my mid-20s. By now I was 32 years old and as much as I wanted to believe things would improve, I was beginning to have doubts. I started the new season in the reserves again. I'd played just one game for the first team, against Derby County, by Christmas and a few games in the UEFA Cup, scoring as a substitute against the Dutch club Twente Enschede. The crowd gave me a tremendous ovation that day, too. I played in both legs of the tie against Standard Liege and in Italy against AC Milan, when the game had been moved to a Thursday afternoon because of fog the previous evening. Generally, though, I was playing in the reserves.

The club had made the 1978–79 season my testimonial year, as was the norm in those days after ten years' service, though I told the chairman of my testimonial committee, Reuben Kay, that I didn't want to attend a string of dinners and other functions in which I'd have to appear in public.

The testimonial match was scheduled for Wednesday, 20 December 1978 but it was postponed on the Monday amid concerns about the weather. City's secretary, Bernard Halford, knew there was a danger of a frozen pitch and fog, which would not be good for the players of City, United, Liverpool and Everton, who'd agreed to play. A new date for the game would be found in 1979.

Early in the New Year, Peter Swales felt that Tony Book needed some help in his attempts to make City a bigger and more successful club than United and a run of disappointing results had prompted an approach to Plymouth Argyle to bring Malcolm Allison back to work with the first team alongside Tony. Malcolm rejoined us on Monday, 8 January, determined to bring back the glory days. As time went on, his role became more and more dominant, as was typical of Malcolm.

It's easy to look back now and say that Malcolm should never have returned but at the time I was happy to see him back at Maine Road. He'd helped make me into the player I was and his faith in me was confirmed three weeks later when he named me as the substitute in an FA Cup tie at Shrewsbury Town.

The game should never have been played. The pitch was frozen solid, which I knew would make things difficult for me. We lost the game 0–2. Malcolm picked me in the starting eleven for the next two league games, the first a trip to White Hart Lane to take on Tottenham and the second the home derby against United.

At Spurs, Malcolm asked me to play sweeper, a role I found easy, even with my restricted movement. I could read the game perfectly from that position. We won 3–0 and I was given the man-of-the-match award, which proved I must have done OK. I stayed in the team for the derby but again the match was played on a frozen pitch.

I played sweeper that day, too, but things didn't go as well as they had done at Tottenham and we lost the game 0–3. The fact that I was made even more immobile by the state of the playing surface told me it was getting close to the point where I might have to consider calling it a day. It was a thought I didn't want to contemplate. Ironically, it had been another game against United that proved to be the beginning of the end for me.

I played in the last seven league games that season, with my last appearance in the first team being a 2–3 defeat at Maine Road against Aston Villa. I knew the end was coming but couldn't make the final decision for myself. I'd fought so long to get back to full fitness that I couldn't face admitting to myself that the battle was over.

I knew I couldn't play like I'd done in the past; it frustrated me and I certainly didn't want to play for another club. If I had to pack it in, there was only one place I was going to do it and that was at Maine Road. I'd enjoyed my three years at Bury but City was the only club for me.

With the summer break now stretching out in front of me, I blocked any doubts out of my mind and still used every spare moment to train. Even at home I would do squats to try to achieve that extra bit of flexibility in the joint. My son, Jon, had been born in October 1978, so pushing the pram to the park gave me another excuse to keep my knee moving.

As the new football season approached, I was trying to convince myself that, despite my doubts, I could carry on playing. However, the possibility that I might have to stop playing had by now been festering in my mind for a while. I wasn't happy with the way I was performing and I didn't want to let people down. Malcolm Allison was starting to build a young team with new signings like Michael Robinson and Steve Mackenzie but he also knew by then that I wouldn't be part of his plans.

Of all the people to make the decision for me, no one seemed more appropriate than Malcolm Allison. He'd been my mentor for so many years, it seemed fitting that he should pull me to one side and tell me it was time to go. We were standing in the players' tunnel at Maine Road when Malcolm told me what I already knew.

Even though I knew he was right and I agreed with what he said, I think I would still be battling to play in the first team now if he hadn't stopped me. Malcolm told me, years later, that telling me I was finished was one of the hardest things he'd ever done.

'You played on after the injury and we could all see that you were never going to get fully fit again. It quickly became apparent that it was wrong for you to carry on. Watching you play made me fall in love with the game more and more. It broke my heart to have to tell you that it was time to finish but there could be no other ending.'

CHAPTER FIFTEEN
What Do I Do Now?

My first duty following the decision to hang up my boots was to inform the supporters via the media. I've never enjoyed talking in public, so you can imagine how difficult it was for me to drive to Maine Road on Tuesday, 21 August 1979 to say my goodbyes.

The whole day felt unreal, from the moment I woke up until I returned home with my kit and boots for the final time. I sat and answered questions from the press, flanked by Peter Swales and Tony Book, who seemed more upset than me. I couldn't help thinking that I should have been able to play on until I was 40 – after all, I was fitter than Booky and he'd experienced the best days of his career after my retirement age.

I didn't want to become a manager, as it seemed too stressful, and I certainly didn't want to carry on playing in the lower divisions. The advice from medical people was to stop trying to return or I could cripple myself for life. I didn't know what I was going to do with my life but I had to accept that it wouldn't include football.

When I arrived home that evening, everything seemed normal. Marie and the kids were there as usual and since football had never really been a topic of conversation at home, nothing had changed. There must have been times when Marie wanted me to quit during those endless months of pounding the streets and going in for treatment. But she knew how much playing football meant to me and there were many times when she kept me going.

Although I knew I wouldn't be able to play in it, my testimonial match had finally been rearranged, so there was still one more occasion to look forward to. The game, Manchester versus Merseyside, took place on Tuesday, 11 September 1979.

Joe Corrigan looked certain to miss the match because he was in Ron Greenwood's England squad to face Denmark at Wembley the following night but once Ray Clemence and Peter Shilton reported with no injury problems, Joe asked for permission to play.

The list of players who'd agreed to take part included City's new signing Steve Daley, Michael Robinson and, of course, Big Joe, with United represented by Lou Macari, Sammy McIlroy and Martin Buchan – the player whose tackle had effectively ended my career. The Merseyside team was to include Jimmy Case, Ray Kennedy and David Johnson from Liverpool, with Brian Kidd, Andy King and Colin Todd from Everton.

I was looking forward to the occasion but was painfully aware that this would be my final farewell. It was another emotional night for me, as over 24,000 fans came to show their appreciation and say goodbye. I walked out to a guard of honour from the players and Joe Corrigan introduced me to all those who'd come to play in the game, including Martin Buchan.

As we shook hands, I wasn't thinking about the night of the

tackle, though I was later told that everyone was watching that moment closely to see how the two of us would react. Since then, many people have asked me how I felt at that time. My simple answer is that I've never blamed him for the tackle that ultimately ended my career, so I was glad to see him again. He'd been a challenging and tough opponent, simple as that.

Manchester won the game 2–1, with the winner coming from young Tommy Caton. Apart from the reception I got from the supporters, the highlight of the evening was probably the penalty shoot-out at half-time, which featured old friends and teammates like Francis Lee and Mike Summerbee along with great rivals from United including Pat Crerand, David Sadler and my hero, Bobby Charlton.

I received no insurance pay-out from the club as they didn't have a policy to protect individual players at that time and I had no personal insurance, so the £30,000 I received from the proceeds of that game, plus the profits from a lottery (to win a Lada car, which was paraded around the ground) was used to start my new life away from football. I believe the winner of the car was involved in an accident a couple of weeks later; the vehicle was written off.

I still had the restaurant in Whitefield and I was now able to spend more of my time at the Bell Waldron. I didn't want to watch City play, so most of the information about how the team was playing came from the supporters, who were our regular customers. It wasn't that I didn't care about City any more; I just couldn't stand the thought of watching and not being able to play.

It had been my intention to go into the club a couple of days each week to do some weight training and perhaps take part in a game of head tennis with the players but I never found the time. I was determined to keep fit and started playing some tennis at my local club, as well as going running whenever I could.

I played a bit of golf, too, and it was at a golf day for Ray Clemence's testimonial in Lymm that I bumped into the former Manchester United player Bill Foulkes. As we chatted, Billy casually asked me if I'd like to play for San Jose Earthquakes in America. He revealed that he was the manager of the team and was trying to recruit players for the new season.

My initial reaction was to say no, because I'd had to retire with the injury. I told him I had restricted movement in the knee, which wasn't going to improve, and I explained that I wasn't the same player he had seen in the early 1970s. He assured me that none of that mattered and he still wanted me to join his club. I wasn't convinced and told Billy I was grateful for the offer but felt I must decline.

When I got home, I told Marie and she immediately suggested I'd made a mistake. She thought playing in the sunshine would do me good and persuaded me to ring Billy and tell him I'd changed my mind.

I flew to California during Easter 1980, accompanied by Marie and Dawn. We left baby Jon with the nanny at home, as Marie planned to stay for only a fortnight. I expected to stay in the United States for their summer season.

We were both impressed with the country from the moment we arrived. The driving was easy, the huge shopping malls were spotless and the people were very friendly. We met some English people who ran a place where we could eat fish and chips and drink a shandy or two.

We also experienced a couple of earthquakes, which, I was told, were quite normal in that area. I wasn't used to seeing chandeliers swaying or ornaments being thrown around the room and found the whole experience a little unnerving. Now I knew why they were called San Jose Earthquakes!

After Marie returned home, I had a flat of my own. On one

away trip, I shared a room with George Best, who'd joined the club soon after me. I don't know who paid his phone bill but he seemed to be on the line to England all the time.

I liked George: he was good company. His wife, Angie, joined him at one stage and I liked her, too. She would regularly entertain us at barbecues at the complex where we were staying. She used to look after George in those days, keeping him away from the drink. After matches, we were regularly invited to parties held for the players, which were attended by party girls and others associated with the club.

People in his company would offer him a beer and Angie would shout up in the background that he'd have an orange juice. I didn't know George very well before I went out there; we'd only really met on match days in the players' lounge. I found him easy to chat to and very down to earth. I never went out drinking with him. I was known for my stamina but I didn't have *that* much! It's sad to see what's happened to him down the years.

As a player, he was something special, as anyone who saw him play will know. He could beat people with his eyes closed. I couldn't do that with mine open! He was always an eye-catching player, making and scoring a lot of goals. Just like Neil Young at City, George had always found football easy, though he certainly didn't go through the motions at San Jose and he wasn't frightened of getting 'stuck in'.

Bill Foulkes asked me to play as a sweeper, as Malcolm had done at City during my last few games. The position suited me. I could read the game and in the slower tempo of American soccer I could do myself justice, though my movement was still as restricted as when I'd retired at City.

I went to clinics and colleges while I was there in a continued attempt to improve the knee. Their medical experts expressed surprise that I'd not had more specialised treatment after the injury and had basically just tried to recover through exercise. Frankly, they seemed stunned that I had, under the circumstances, even been able to walk again, let alone play football.

I knew within days that I was going to enjoy the lifestyle out there. Everything started so well but I then became unsettled by a comment made to me by the former Tottenham player Alfie Conn, before I'd even played a game. Alfie had joined us in California. He told me on the coach, on the way to that first match, that I was on a 'waiver'. I asked him what that meant and he told me that my name had been circulated to other clubs as a potential transfer signing.

After the game, I went to see Billy and told him straight that I hadn't gone to the States to switch from one club to another. I told him that if *he* didn't want me, I'd be on the first plane home. All he could say in reply was, 'That's just the way it is in football over here.' I wasn't happy with his response but decided to carry on – for the time being, at least.

The chap who held the franchise for San Jose Earthquakes was Milan Mandaric, who went on to become the chairman of Portsmouth. He was so impressed by my performance in one game in Vancouver that he said I could have anything I wanted and that nothing would be too much trouble. That seemed to be the kiss of death: I think I was on my way home a fortnight later.

The names over our pegs at training used to change on an almost daily basis. Some bloke, who was a dead-ringer for Jerry Lewis, would replace one name with another and chuckle, 'Do you want the good news or the bad news?' One player came in from Portugal and only lasted one day before he moved on. It seemed a strange way to run a football club.

After just half a dozen games during my six weeks in America,

I decided I'd had enough and returned home. This time my football career really was, finally, over.

Once I'd returned from the United States, I gave my full attention to the Bell Waldron and enjoyed the extra responsibility of running the restaurant on a day-to-day basis. We had a great Spanish head chef, Tino Chevez, and very attentive staff. Our meals were reasonably priced so although the restaurant was a success, it wasn't hugely profitable. I didn't want the diners to be 'ripped off'; I wanted them to eat good, quality food at a reasonable price.

After years of planning my life around football, I was now determined to make sure everything centred on my family. My children were growing up and I made sure I was with them every step of the way. I did the school run with Dawn and Jon every morning and I don't think I ever missed a parents' evening.

Dawn played hockey and tennis as she grew older and Jon represented Cheshire at rugby. As a parent, I showed the same commitment to both of them, watching them play their respective sports as much as I could.

I tried to be as anonymous as possible on the touchline and I'm sure most of the other parents didn't even notice I was there. I didn't try to push either of them. It had been their choice to take part in sport and they played the sports they enjoyed.

It might have seemed more natural for Jon to be a footballer than a rugby player but I never deterred him. He played football for a while at junior level and was usually asked to play as a central defender, because he was taller than the other kids of his age. He was quite good but when he chose to play rugby, his preferred sport, I had no objections.

Soon after I'd returned from the States, a City fan called Alan Ridgeway asked me to judge a beauty contest at the Butlins Holiday Camp in Scarborough. I had time on my hands, so I accepted the invitation and enjoyed the trip. That, in turn, led to an invitation to do some coaching during the summers that followed at the various camps around the country, including Bognor, Skegness and Minehead.

I enjoyed being involved in football again and I used to spend two days at each camp working with the youngsters. They also invited Marie and me to Blackpool and Scarborough to judge the finals of competitions like the 'Glamorous Granny'. We enjoyed ourselves doing things like that.

That was the pattern of our lives for a few years. I didn't watch much football and was barely aware of what was happening. I played an occasional round of golf with Alan Oakes, Glyn Pardoe or Mike Doyle and chatted now and again to Tony Book, but my working life centred on the restaurant and my trips to Butlins.

By 1989, the Bell Waldron had run its course and was beginning to struggle in the face of fierce competition from restaurant chains that were starting to spring up all over the place. I was still convinced that the quality of the evening we were offering was better but it was becoming more difficult to make a profit.

I'd opened the restaurant as my insurance policy for a 'rainy day' and had never really imagined that it would keep me going for so long. I decided that, after 20 years, it was time to sell up and move on to something else. We sold the premises that year and it eventually became a Balti House. For the second time in my life, I had to make a big career change.

My life in football had made us financially secure but I needed a fresh challenge. I had no idea what it would be. For a while, I had time on my hands. I played some golf and tennis at the local club and would take our dog, Sam, out for long walks. One day, I got a call from Willie Donachie, who was the assistant manager at Oldham Athletic with Joe Royle, and he asked me to meet him at Boundary Park.

Willie invited me to watch a couple of training sessions with a view to me becoming involved on the coaching side. Ken Barnes, City's great half-back from the 1950s, and father of Peter Barnes, was the chief scout at City and had heard I'd been up at Oldham, so he asked me to call in and see him at Maine Road.

Once he became aware that I might get more involved at Oldham, he became determined to make sure I used my experience to help City. Ken asked me to come down to the ground and join the social gatherings that took place in his office. They were very informal and never at a set time.

Ken knew everyone and among those who popped in from time to time were Denis Law and City old-boys like Steve Fleet and Roy Cheetham. Other visitors to Ken's office included former United player Dennis Viollet and even the United manager Alex Ferguson – though I was never there at the same time as him.

We'd talk about whatever had happened during the last few days, while drinking tea. It was my way of keeping up to date with what was going on. Ken also asked me to call in at one or two training sessions with the club's youngsters just to give an opinion or pass on a bit of advice. That was how it was for quite a few months.

One day, Barnesy asked me if I wanted to get involved with the club, on the youth side, on a more formal basis. I leapt at the chance.

Initially, he asked me to do some scouting and to coach City's 'B' team but gradually the role grew. He asked me to assess the strengths of the young players and to come into the club two or three days a week. I felt the role suited me perfectly. It was great to be involved at City again. I'd rejoined my other family.

Howard Kendall was the City manager at that time and eventually Barnesy asked Kendall if I could be brought officially onto the staff, which would mean I'd receive a modest salary. It wasn't much but that didn't matter to me. I didn't have a specific title or role but just over a decade after I'd retired as a player at City, I was back.

CHAPTER SIXTEEN
Back at Manchester City

It was great being back at City and before very long I was working every available hour, though I never complained. It's great when you do a job you love. I never discussed the wages, so even when my official hours increased from one day a week to four days, I never went into the office demanding more money.

I was told that one of the requirements of the job was to have a coaching badge, so, naturally, I started the process of qualifying. I was convinced I'd fail. As soon as the tutors started talking, I was lost and didn't really understand what they were trying to tell me. There was so much theory that I would easily get confused. The fact that I had played the game at the top level seemed to count for nothing.

The practical side of the coaching was never a problem. Running sessions and talking to players was easy but the written tests were another matter. English had never been one of my strengths at school and, anyway, isn't football supposed to be a simple game?

During the last part of the written exam, which was on refereeing, the adjudicator left us unsupervised in the room for a while. Naturally, we all discussed what the best answers would be. I think the examiner left us alone on purpose so we'd work out the answers together.

Even the practical part of the exam had sections that I thought were daft. One day we had been told by our instructor that when you stop a group of players from running you can't shout, 'Hold it'. I did. He stopped the session and walked over to me. He told me that I had to use the word 'Stop' and not any other word. *He'd* stopped the session by saying, 'Hold it there', to tell me off for shouting 'Hold it'! Malcolm Allison had *never* shouted 'Stop' at us during training and it had never done us any harm.

I suppose that type of incident happens in all walks of life. In my restaurant, we used to get people applying to work in our kitchens with every qualification you could imagine. Our way of deciding whether they were what we wanted was to get them to work with the head chef for a couple of weeks and see how they did. That seemed a much more sensible way of assessing their suitability and I believe that's how it should be done in life. Certificates don't mean anything to me. We never made any bad choices in the restaurant, so it clearly worked for us.

I'm not sure how, but I passed my coaching certificate so I was able to satisfy all the legal requirements of my job at City, although my main role wasn't really coaching. Most of my time was spent scouting and acting as a link between the families of the young players and the club. I could chat through any problems they had because I had been through it myself as a youngster.

I knew all about growing spurts and being away from home, and I felt I had all the right skills to help them through their problems. I used to work with Terry Farrell, who was well read on all the rules and regulations. He was also a very good organiser. He knew the area really well and had scouts all over the place. He knew all there was to know about signing young players, training them and looking after their welfare. I was his right-hand man.

As well as working with the youngsters, I was also asked to give my opinion on players that the club was considering signing. I went to an England Under-15s game against Scotland and I remember asking Terry (Farrell) the name of the No. 10 for England. It was Michael Owen. I asked Terry if the lad was on the books of a professional club and he told me he was with Liverpool.

He was such a good player that I still wondered if there was any way of getting him to City. Every week for a year or so, I kept trying to persuade Terry to find a way of signing him. I even jokingly suggested I became his agent, so I could persuade him to sign for City. I remember watching him score a hat-trick against United's youth team, years later, and thinking, 'If only'.

Another player who made an immediate impact on me was Michael Brown, who came down from Hartlepool to have a trial. Soon after seeing him in action at Platt Lane I spoke to his father and asked him if he'd like to come to City. Peter Reid had recommended Brown and I knew from seeing him in one game that he would be a very good player. As well as playing in City's first team, he went on to play in an FA Cup semi-final for Sheffield United and in the Premiership for Tottenham Hotspur.

Lee Crooks and Chris Greenacre were among the others that caught my eye and Garry Flitcroft particularly impressed me. I spoke to Garry after a youth-team game at Chorley against Bolton. I didn't feel he'd made as much of an impression in the game as he should have. I told him he was in a different class to the others in the team but that he hadn't imposed himself enough.

It was a similar situation with Steve Lomas when he played for our 'A' team in a game at Morecambe against their reserves. I'd warned the whole team that the opposition would be fired up because they were playing against Manchester City but we were still beaten 2–4.

Typically, Steve was the type of youngster who wouldn't shirk a tackle but he'd gone missing in that game. I saw him a few days later and asked him if he'd been unwell. I encouraged him to be more aggressive, as I saw that as his number one strength. I didn't need to tell Steve twice.

I spent hours driving up and down the motorways to Scotland, personally checking the recommendations made by the scouts. I believe you should judge a player in his own environment whenever possible. I used to tell the other scouts that if they believed in a player they shouldn't give up the chase just because he had a bad game now and again.

I had a very good relationship with the scouts. I remember one of them, a gentleman called Willie Thompson, trying to give me a bottle of whisky, which he explained was a token of his appreciation for the help I'd given him. I felt uncomfortable and didn't want to take it. As far as I was concerned, I was doing a job I loved for my football club and I didn't feel it was appropriate to receive a gift in that way. He wouldn't take no for an answer, so eventually I accepted the gift and his thanks. I've probably still got that bottle of whisky somewhere, unopened.

After a few years during which I fulfilled various roles, including coaching the 'B' team and becoming joint youth development officer with Terry Farrell, Ken Barnes retired and the office he had once occupied became our base. I wasn't one for being based in an office, though, and I spent as much time as possible out on the pitch with the youngsters or driving up and down the country either meeting parents or scouting.

By early 1994, I had been back at the club for four years and had loved every minute. I've never been interested in the politics within the club but I was aware that there had been a long battle for control at board level. However, just as in my playing days, I hadn't got involved – I just concentrated on doing my best for City.

There had been protests by supporters against chairman Peter Swales and plenty of newspaper stories about what was going on but as far as I was concerned it didn't affect me.

Mr Swales had been reluctant to give up control of the club but I don't think he should have been hounded out like he was. No one should be treated like that. Perhaps he should have stepped down or moved aside more graciously once it became obvious things weren't going the way he wanted. He probably needed to take the blinkers off and see he wasn't doing a good job any more.

During my playing days, I didn't need people to tell me I'd had a bad game; I knew. Peter Swales was a blue through and through, a big supporter and City mad. I think, in the end, he became too close to the playing side, which proved to be a big mistake.

My old friend, Francis Lee, eventually took over as chairman in February that year and I was happy to see him back. We'd never been as close as the supporters had imagined, so I didn't expect any favours and his arrival didn't affect my working day in any way.

I respected Francis and, along with the other great players from our era, we'd had some great times together but that was as far as it went. I had every confidence that Francis returning to the club would have a positive effect on everyone; after all, he was one of the City 'family'.

Changes happen frequently at football clubs. Players come and go and there had been many comings and goings among the backroom staff, too, with former manager Jimmy Frizzell taking over as chief scout and ex-player Neil McNab becoming part of the coaching staff.

I'd been with Jimmy to watch Gio Kinkladze play for Georgia against Wales. Kinkladze had orchestrated the game and sent a great chip-shot just over the crossbar. Jimmy asked my opinion on the player and I told him I was impressed. He told me we could sign the player for £500,000 and asked me if I thought that would be good value for money. I told him it would be well worth the risk to sign him for that amount.

A few weeks later, the club bought him for £2 million. I've never understood why the fee went up so much between that first assessment and the day we signed him.

Although I wasn't involved with the first team, I was aware of the rapid turnover of managers that happened during the next three years, with Brian Horton, Alan Ball and Steve Coppell all having spells in charge plus various others on a short-term basis. I just carried on doing what I knew I could do best, never craving the spotlight and happy in the background.

I have always believed that young players need to be encouraged and praised. As boys grow through their teenage years, their personalities are complex and their confidence can be fragile. I believe the best results are therefore achieved through patience.

Inevitably, there comes a time in the career of most youngsters when a decision has to be made as to whether they are good enough or not. Only a small percentage go on to be successful and highly paid; the rest drop away and never make it. Even though it is often possible to identify those who will make it and those who won't at an early stage, I believe all the young players should be treated with equal respect and that an open mind should be kept throughout the process.

Neil McNab had a different approach to me and he treated the youngsters as if they were adults playing in the first team. I didn't approve of the way he talked to the boys. His style didn't seem appropriate for youngsters, though I'm sure it wouldn't have been out of place in a senior dressing-room.

I found McNab a difficult person to deal with. He disagreed with my view of how things should be done and seemed determined to undermine my authority as youth development officer. There were a series of incidents that seemed designed to embarrass me and I observed a number of things that made me feel he wasn't representing my club in the right way.

He seemed to resent me, which I couldn't understand. It appeared that he had a serious and deep problem in relating to me within the club and I thought he might have felt intimidated by my name and the great success I'd had as a player. I had never sought to use my name to further my career and I have never expected any favours.

After many years of happiness at Manchester City, for the first time in my life I dreaded going into the club. I was deeply unhappy and didn't know what to do. I wasn't the only person who felt that way but I became more and more frustrated and couldn't see a solution to the problem.

On a couple of occasions, I requested meetings with Francis Lee, the highest authority at the club, and told him of my concerns about Neil McNab. He didn't react to my complaints in the way I'd hoped, simply telling me he'd consider the matter and decide what to do about it. A couple of weeks later, I was told McNab had been offered a new two-year contract, which gave me my answer.

In January 1997, Frank Clark came in as the new manager and I saw this as a perfect opportunity to air my concerns again. Terry Farrell and I went to see him and he seemed sympathetic to our point of view. Despite several meetings with Frank Clark and his assistant, Alan Hill, nothing changed.

On 8 May, Terry and I represented the club at a meeting of youth staff from all over the North-west, to look back on the previous season and look ahead to the next. The meeting took place at Maine Road. During one of the breaks, I bumped into Ken Barnes, who told me that Frank Clark wanted to see Terry and me at the Platt Lane complex.

Once the meeting of youth staff ended, we went along, as requested, with Terry going in to see Frank Clark first. A few minutes later, Terry emerged to tell me he'd been sacked. I hadn't expected that and my head was still spinning when I took my turn to face Frank Clark and Alan Hill.

I'd barely sat down when, in a clinical and cold way, Clark simply said, 'We're dispensing with your services.' I asked him if it was *their* decision. They simply replied, 'We've made the decision.' The only explanation I was given was that they wanted to 'sort out the department'. Neil McNab was also sacked that day.

The termination of my employment came as a deep shock. I had not received the slightest indication that it was likely to happen. Terry and I had never heard a word of complaint nor had we ever received a warning in regard to our performance or the conduct of the department.

The youth team had an excellent record, finishing top, joint top and in third place during the previous three seasons. I'd attended a meeting of the Prestwich and Whitefield Supporters Group less than a week earlier, with Alan Hill, where we'd received a cheque from the fans towards youth development.

They'd been full of praise for the progress that had been made.

Francis Lee made no attempt to contact me in the aftermath of the dismissal and he has publicly claimed to have been in Jersey when I was sacked. He has repeatedly said he had nothing to do with the decision. If I had been the chairman of Manchester City when a decision of that nature had been taken, I would have done things differently.

I felt Francis Lee let my family and me down very badly. I didn't expect any favours but I feel the manner in which I was treated was wrong.

My family and I felt humiliated by what had happened, despite many letters of support from the fans. I'd expected to see out the rest of my working life with City. I reluctantly asked for the return of my England cap, which had been loaned to the club for display. It broke my heart to take it back but I felt it was something I had to do.

I've never been comfortable pushing myself into the public eye, but I decided that I had to speak out in some way to clear my name and repair my damaged reputation. I took legal advice with a view to taking the club to an employment tribunal. I saw it as an opportunity to make my concerns public in an unbiased way. I didn't take the decision lightly and the last thing I wanted was to harm Manchester City but I felt it was the only way I could let the supporters know what had gone on.

The case came to court in mid-October. Francis Lee did not attend. I'd wanted him to appear in court so that I could hear his side of the story. The court case didn't run long enough for that to happen. After hearing detailed accounts of what had taken place during the last year of my time at City, the chairman of the tribunal suggested that the club and our legal representatives settled the matter out of court, which we did.

I felt that proved Terry and I had been in the right, although

I would have preferred the court proceedings to have gone on longer so that more details of the situation could have emerged.

Later that year, on 17 October to be precise, the *Manchester Evening News*, reporting on the club's AGM, which was attended by my nephew and father-in-law, stated that Francis Lee defended the decision to sack me. Apparently, he was pressed by irate shareholders, in particular a gentleman called Brian Williams, who was cheered when he described my dismissal as 'a disgrace'.

I'm reluctant to go into any great detail about what happened during that horrible last year I spent at City. It would serve no purpose now and I care too much about Manchester City to say anything that would cause potential harm. What I will say is that I no longer have any contact with Francis Lee.

Mike Summerbee has tried to act as a go-between and peacemaker, and he often brings me items, such as shirts and pictures, signed by Francis Lee, for me to add my autograph to. As long as they're for charity I have no problem in doing it, but I have decided that I will not attend any function at which Francis Lee is present.

I am a forgiving person but I am also stubborn. This is one occasion when I will stand resolutely by my decision.

CHAPTER SEVENTEEN
After Football

At the age of 51, my life in football was finally over – but what a career to look back on. It had certainly been full of ups and downs but I wouldn't change a thing. I spent the first few months of my enforced retirement handling all the paperwork surrounding the court case. I certainly wasn't in the right frame of mind to go and watch City play, though I had plenty of friends who kept me informed about what was going on.

I'd always had a life away from football, of course, but that had run side by side with my love of the game, which, for most of my life, had been with Manchester City. I have always said that I have two families, the one at home with Marie, Jon and Dawn and the other, my football club.

I am still involved in sport. I'm a member of my local tennis club in Hale Barns, playing doubles matches in the local league and occasional cup ties. The courts at Hale Barns are Astroturf, which helps my knee cope with the twisting and turning because the surface has a little bit more 'give' in it.

I'm also a member of Hale Golf Club but play the sport more

for leisure than competition. The only golf event I've ever been involved in was their Winter Doubles competition – which I won, partnered by a friend called Bernard Elliott.

I ran in four marathons during the 1980s, my best time, despite the dodgy knee, being three hours eleven minutes. I'd been advised not to run in events of that nature because of the pounding the knee would take but I wanted to run anyway. These days there are problems with both my knees. All the running I've done since the injury has caused damage on the left side, due to over-compensation.

As I've said before, I'm stubborn and it's my nature to keep fit and compete. I've always been keen to help those less fortunate than myself and I used those events as a way of raising money for various charities, including Brookvale Jewish Children's Home in Prestwich, Mencap, the NSPCC and Genesis.

I've also been invited to play in pro-celebrity tennis tournaments, such as the Direct Line International Ladies' Tennis Championships in Eastbourne, where I played alongside Sir Cliff Richard, Mike Read and the musician Jeff Wayne. Top women players, including Natalie Tauziat, Jana Novotna and Arantxa Sanchez Vicario, also took part and I thoroughly enjoyed the whole experience.

Whenever I'm asked to take part in any tennis event I always donate my fee to the Lorna Fogarty Tennis Trust, which supports tennis in inner-city schools; in fact, I've also passed a tennis coaching certificate, so I can go and help the youngsters directly.

Just over a year after I'd been sacked by City, and with my club now newly relegated to Division Two, Francis Lee stepped down as chairman. He was replaced by David Bernstein, with another of my old teammates, Dennis Tueart, also joining the board. Dennis contacted my close friend and mentor Ian Wilson, who'd acted as my solicitor during the employment tribunal, to set up a meeting between Dennis, Mr Bernstein, Ian and myself.

Dennis felt I had suffered an injustice and wanted to get me back involved at the club. At the meeting it was suggested that I work in the corporate suites at Maine Road on a match day. They wanted me to meet the supporters who were enjoying pre-match meals and discuss football with them and generally make them feel at home. I'd done a fair bit of that during my days at the Bell Waldron, so it was something I felt I could do.

I still find it quite difficult to walk up to complete strangers and introduce myself, even after all the years of doing that at the restaurant and at City on match days. I'm always flattered when someone says that I was their hero or that they enjoyed watching me play, but I still feel awkward interrupting their meal or starting a conversation. I'm sure some people think I'm aloof or arrogant but that is certainly not the case; I've never forgotten my humble roots.

May 1999 proved to be a terrific month for me. First I was invited to attend the 'Football League Evening of Legends', which was held at the Hilton Hotel in London on the 13th. The Football Association and Sportswriters had selected the 100 best footballers of the twentieth century and I was named alongside great players like Stanley Matthews, Nat Lofthouse, George Best, Tom Finney, Joe Mercer, Gordon Banks, Bobby Moore and Alan Ball, just to mention a few.

There must be hundreds of great players that weren't included. For example, my top left-back of all time, Ray Wilson, was missing. Some of my biggest heroes were on the list, though, including my top two, Bobby Charlton and Len Shackleton.

There were five players selected for their contributions while at City – Bert Trautmann, Billy Meredith, Peter Doherty (father of Paul Doherty who'd recommended me to City all those years ago and become such a good friend), Frank Swift and me. What an honour. I treasure the medal they gave me that night as highly as anything I ever received as a player.

It was a great evening mixing with so many of those great names from the past. Later that month, I was invited into the Royal Box at Wembley, to see the play-off final against Gillingham. Just like all the other supporters who were there that day, I wondered how City had dropped so far down the leagues. It seemed like only yesterday to me that we were being presented with the FA Cup in the same stadium.

Watching a football match when you've been a player is never easy. You kick every ball and head every cross. I was as frustrated as ever that day that I couldn't be out there helping my team win. On a day like that, as I watched City come from behind in injury time against Gillingham, I would have done anything to be out there playing for City again.

It was a big relief seeing Nicky Weaver save that final penalty from Guy Butters, which won the shootout and got us back into Division One. What a great month it had turned out to be. Typical of City, certainly in recent seasons, I witnessed some good games and some bad ones during the next couple of years, during which the club was promoted again the following season, before coming straight back down in May 2001.

The new season saw Kevin Keegan, another of my former teammates (albeit only briefly, with England), take over as manager. His first season in charge was marvellous, the football was great and it was very pleasing to see the team deservedly win the Second Division title . . . I can't get used to all the different names they keep giving the different divisions.

I know it was called the First Division and these days it's known as the Championship, but why they have to keep messing around with the names of the divisions is beyond me.

When I hear the results on a Saturday, it sometimes takes a few minutes to work out which division a particular team is in!

Ironically, the trophy Kevin Keegan's team received for winning the First Division was the same one we won back in 1968 at Newcastle. As far as I'm concerned, they earned their success by playing good football, with an emphasis on attacking.

That summer, in 2002, Manchester staged the Commonwealth Games and I was given the honour of carrying the baton on a leg of the Queen's Jubilee Baton Relay. I only ran with the baton for a few hundred yards but I was proud to be involved.

The following season was the last to be played at Maine Road. I'm not an emotional person but naturally there were times when someone would be talking about the games played back in the 1960s and '70s that would make me think back.

I remember having a picture taken with Eyal Berkovic in one of the stands a couple of weeks before the final game against Southampton. I don't think he had any idea who I was, not that it bothered me.

During the week before the final game, I listened to a radio documentary about Maine Road, made by Ian Cheeseman, on BBC GMR. Marie, Jon and I listened to the full three hours and that was the closest I came to shedding a tear.

On the day of the final game, Sunday, 11 May 2003, I was asked to be one of the guests of honour alongside Malcolm Allison and Joe Mercer's widow, Norah Mercer. To be bracketed with those two was something special. I was presented to the two teams before kick-off, which was another great honour. I remember suggesting to some of the Southampton players that they should save themselves for the following week's FA Cup final, which was much more important.

I said to the City goalkeeper Peter Schmeichel, who I knew

was retiring, that it would have been nice if he'd hung up his gloves after the game at Anfield a few days earlier, when his great saves had helped City win there for the first time since the early 1980s. One of the saves he made that day was among the best I've ever seen. I could understand why he'd wanted to finish in the last game at Maine Road, though.

I can't remember what I said to Shaun Goater but I know I also spoke to Shaun Wright-Phillips, Nicolas Anelka and Niclas Jensen. There were a lot of thoughts flashing around in my head because it was the last time I would ever go to the old ground that held so many memories for me.

To see supporters upset and crying, obviously with *their* memories to the fore, was very emotional, even for me. I'm sure, though, that the whole occasion meant more to the supporters than it did to me.

I always loved the size of the Maine Road pitch, which allowed me to use my fitness to get away from whoever was marking me. The groundsmen rightly won an award for the quality of the playing surface during that final season. It was like a bowling green.

I saw a bit of the pop concert that was staged after the game but I have to admit I'm not a big music fan, though I've always liked Elvis Presley. That part of the farewell to Maine Road wasn't for me. The day was all about the final match and about the memories. I suppose it will be seen as 'typical City' that we lost that final game 0–1. In recent years, the team always seems to have done the unexpected.

Even during my time, I remember us being unpredictable on occasions and making hard work of things that should have been quite straightforward. We played Wigan in an FA Cup tie at Maine Road in 1971 before they came into the league. When you get a draw like that, you tend to assume it'll be easy. What you can easily forget is that teams like that always come out of the traps running, pushing and chasing.

It's their cup final and I remember that being a very hard game. We won it 1–0 in the end but they wouldn't let us play the football we were used to. One of the lessons we learnt that day was that one of the most important parts of being a footballer is getting the mental side right.

As far as that last match at Maine Road is concerned, I missed a lot of it. I never saw any of the 'parade of legends'. I was doing my match-day job, walking around the tables on the top floor of the Kippax Stand. A lot of people had made a point of asking me to go and chat with them because of the occasion.

I'd been looking forward to seeing a lot of the older players who I knew had been invited to the game. Sadly, apart from seeing Wyn Davies, Tony Towers and Stan Horne, I missed them all. I hardly recognised Tony Towers, whose nickname had been 'Growler'. His hair had gone totally white.

I was particularly disappointed I didn't see Alan Oakes and Mike Doyle. I was also disappointed that only the so-called important players were introduced to the crowd. To me, if they played for Manchester City, they are all important.

After the game, the supporters, naturally, were hanging around outside the ground for hours, just trying to see people leaving for the final time. A couple of security guards were asked to walk me to my car. I don't really enjoy that kind of thing because I don't like to walk away from people if they're asking me to sign autographs.

The security men stayed with me for the first 30 or 40 yards until the initial frenzy was over and there were only a handful of fans left. I asked the security guards to go back at that point. That seemed to prompt another wave of well-wishers, so in the end I stood there for about 45 minutes signing shirts, postcards, programmes – you name it.

I was starting to watch a lot more football by now. Naturally, I saw all of City's home games and I also watched quite a few games on TV, usually with my son, Jon. I'm not sure if the way the game has changed is for the better. It disappoints me that there are so many non-British players in the Premiership.

When I retired from playing and went to play for San Jose Earthquakes for a while, they were trying to get football off the ground over there. They had to play three Americans, and I liked that rule. I think there should be a rule like that over here now. I don't think our national team is helped by the current situation.

I'm disappointed by the England national team. There only seem to be about 15 quality players in the squad and there are plenty that are not good enough. There must be players from my day who wonder why they never got an England cap, especially when they see how easily they are handed out these days. There are too many friendlies and far too many substitutions. England caps should have to be earned, not handed out like confetti.

If you're English and play for a top-four Premiership club you seem to be an automatic choice to play for your country, which says a lot about the way the game has changed, in a way that isn't very healthy for our national game. I would rather see the England squad being made up of players drawn from clubs throughout the top flight.

For years, England has struggled to find a left-sided player. In the 1960s and 1970s, you could have picked six different England sides, in all positions, and the weakest eleven would still have been a good side.

I don't like the way today's footballers are so hyped. The media, particularly Sky TV, has created an appetite for football from people who are not really interested in the game as a sport.

The top clubs, these days, generally achieve success with

foreign players in all the key positions. We probably help every other country to have top-quality national teams. It frustrates me when I see players diving about and taking their shirts off when they score a goal. Scoring a goal is just one part of the game and has happened for hundreds of years.

Anybody would think that every goal scored these days is the best there has ever been. I scored plenty of goals and there's no doubt it's the nicest part of the game, but to me it was just as satisfying to win an important tackle. You wouldn't take your shirt off to celebrate winning a tackle, would you? I never used to get emotional scoring a goal, I'd just turn around and think, 'That's it; I've done it'!

The art of tackling seems to have been lost. I've seen plenty of so-called great goals that come from situations where defenders have stood off an opposing player. It's also rare that you see managers asking one of their players to stop a specific opponent from playing. Defending is as important as attacking but these days we only seem to celebrate the offensive aspects of the game.

Charlton Athletic, under Alan Curbishley, is one of the few teams I have seen do this well in recent years. Malcolm Allison always used to make sure we knew how to attack and defend. Malcolm would identify a key player from the opposition, like Alan Ball, and effectively sacrifice one of our players to make sure he didn't have an influential game.

People often ask me if players are overpaid now. They probably are but good luck to them. It's not the player's fault if someone offers them a big contract. However, if you asked me if I'd prefer to be playing today, then my answer would be no.

I can't deny that I would have preferred the wages they are paid and I would have preferred to play on the perfect pitches they have these days but I wouldn't want to swap the way the game was structured. The top flight was far more competitive and it was much harder to predict individual results and who would win the major trophies.

Football was professional in those days too but it always felt more like a sport than perhaps it does today. The major downside of the modern game is the high wages that are paid and the negative influence of agents. I can't help thinking that the edge has been taken off the will to win and that loyalty is no longer important. Winning for our club and its supporters was everything, both to me and to the great players I played alongside and against.

CHAPTER EIGHTEEN
Colin Bell MBE

One of the questions I am asked most frequently these days is, 'How's the knee?' It still doesn't bend back fully but I still consider myself fit and, although it's far from perfect, I will resist an operation to replace the knee-joint for as long as possible. The other knee has deteriorated over the years, too, as I've relied on it more and more.

My sister Eileen and her husband Bart still live in Hesleden and I see them occasionally, though these days it's usually in Hale Barns or Sale rather than the North-east. They visit their son, Keith, who lives in Sale. Keith and I spent so much time together as children that I think of him as my younger brother. He is married to Claire and they have two children, Olivia and James.

I see or speak to Keith every week and from time to time we play golf together. Because of the age gap, he idolised me when I became a successful footballer and he was desperate to follow in my footsteps.

He didn't make it as a footballer but he did fairly well for himself as a cricketer. He'd obviously learnt a lot from our early years together when I'd sent him running around the backyard in Hesleden! Keith became a very useful batsman for the Minor Counties side, Cheshire, as well as his local team at Bowden. He played until his mid-40s. Ironically, he would probably have played on for longer but for a knee injury.

My daughter, Dawn, went to Oxford University from where she graduated with a Masters Degree in mathematics. She must have inherited her mathematical brain from me, because it was my favourite subject at school and I excel at Su Doku. These days she's a successful risk manager, based in the City of London, living near Westminster. She recently got engaged to Jonathan and we're all looking forward to the wedding in Mauritius.

Both my children excelled at school. During their teenage years Marie and I would speak in whispered tones and use sign language, so we wouldn't disturb them as they did their homework. Dawn became Deputy Head Girl at Withington High School and Jon was Head Boy at Stockport Grammar School. Dawn and I spent a lot of time playing board games when she was very young and I'd never let her win, on purpose. She's used that determination to progress through all sorts of exams. She's definitely a winner now.

Jon recently completed his qualifications to become a doctor. His name is followed by the letters BSc MBChB(Hons), which sounds very impressive. Even I don't know what they stand for! He's training as a surgeon at the Manchester Royal Infirmary, having spent three years at St Andrews University in Scotland and three more years at Manchester University to complete his medical degrees. I don't know whether Jon was inspired to be a surgeon because of all the time I'd spent in hospital having operations and recovering from my injuries.

Jon's a big City fan and is very proud of my achievements with the club. At times, he gets a bit frustrated with me because I rarely accept the invitations I receive to go to premières and other such glittering functions. If I have a choice between an evening mixing with the great and good or being with my family or my close friends, I'd always choose the latter.

Jon has also tried to persuade me to do TV interviews but I always say no. He knows I'm a stubborn so-and-so but he still tries to talk me into it. I've never felt comfortable in the limelight and I think it's too late for me to change now.

I spend as much of my free time as I can in the South of France, where we have a holiday home. I've always taken part in the tennis tournament down there. I have to admit that there were some tense moments during those competitions in years gone by. Playing in mixed doubles with your daughter as your partner is a bit like teaching your wife to drive – a recipe for disaster.

Dawn and I are always desperate to win anything we take part in and have a tendency to blame each other if things go wrong. At one time, we vowed we'd never play together again but thankfully that didn't last very long.

I've also spent some of my time during the last few years helping Marie's parents with their family business. I don't mind what I do to help people and I'm certainly not too proud to get my hands dirty. Marie's parents have taken the place of my own.

I'm still very much in love with Marie; I can't imagine life without her. I still struggle to tell her how much I love her. I've never been a tactile person, preferring to give a firm handshake than a hug, but I think I've inherited some of her warmth over the years.

My relationship with the fantastic supporters of Manchester City has never been better. I receive invitations to attend Supporters Club branches on a regular basis and it never ceases to amaze me how affectionately they welcome me. It's been 30 years since I suffered the injury that effectively ended my career and yet the fans talk as if it was yesterday.

2004 was a particularly good year for the family and me. It began when I was inducted into City's Hall of Fame on 22nd January and then, a fortnight later, the West Stand at the City of Manchester Stadium was officially renamed the 'Colin Bell Stand'. I'd thought my great days were far behind me, and of course they are as a player, but the way the supporters honoured me that year was as rewarding as anything that happened during my playing days.

It's difficult to find the words that sum up how I feel about being named in the Hall of Fame, alongside great players like Peter Doherty, Bert Trautmann, Frank Swift, Roy Paul and the rest. It was particularly special for me to receive the award from my old teammate and fellow inductee Tony Book.

The naming of the stand at the City of Manchester Stadium was the pinnacle. The process started when the supporters clubs were asked to suggest possible names. Once a shortlist had been created, the final decision was made via the club's website, where thousands of votes were cast on-line. It was a tremendous honour to be told that my name had won by an overwhelming margin and that the stand, on the side where the teams emerge, was to be renamed the Colin Bell Stand.

Accompanied by Marie and Jon, we ceremonially opened the newly named stand before the game against Birmingham City on 8 February. The chairman, John Wardle, and my old mate Kevin Keegan congratulated me as we posed for some pictures in front of 'my stand', which now proudly carries my name on the front edge of the second tier, inside the stadium. I really love our new home and to look back from the pitch and see my name there is an indescribable feeling.

I would like to have played on the perfect playing surface and been involved in the modern game – I'm sure I would still have held my own – but I have many concerns about the way the game has developed.

During the era in which I played, most teams had the potential to win the League Championship and the major cup competitions. These days money has become the dominant factor, with the emergence of Chelsea providing the perfect example of the way things have moved on.

Every club had three or four great players in the '60s and '70s. These days, if a great player emerges, like Steve Gerrard at Liverpool or Shaun Wright-Phillips at City, it is seen as only a matter of time before they move to one of the biggest three or four clubs, the only ones who are seen to be capable of winning the major honours.

I think it is a sad state of affairs that those types of players don't think that they can fulfil their dreams at the clubs who encouraged them to meet their potential. It never occurred to me that I would have to move away from City. I was a City player for life and my ambitions were to win trophies with my club. I expected to work for success and not simply move on to a club that had already achieved it. It never crossed my mind that I would reach a certain stage and then feel that it was inevitable I move on.

I hope things will change soon and that Manchester City will be able to compete for the top honours again with a group of players who are loyal and care about the club they play for. I wonder if the days when football was more sport than industry will ever return. I've been blessed with such wonderful memories of my days playing for City and having been part of such a great family. We're very close and I spend a lot of time talking to Jon about my favourite subject, football, and in particular Manchester City.

Working on the book has provided me with many opportunities to reflect on my life. Even dropping Jon off at Manchester Airport one day made me recall the many varied experiences I had flying to and from some of the tournaments and games I played in. Naturally, I always think back to our pilot taxiing around the airport in Poland, looking for solid ground and seeing fire engines waiting to meet us as we drank champagne whilst returning from another European adventure, oblivious to any problems on board.

Other experiences include my first flight, when, as a teenager at Bury, we flew to Düsseldorf in Germany. The wings of the aircraft, which had propellers rather than jet engines, seemed too long. Walking down the centre aisle was like walking up a ladder that had been laid on the floor, as there were metal ridges every foot or so. I'm sure the wings flapped as we took off.

With England, we dived so dramatically on an internal flight in South America to pass under a severe storm that the overhead lockers were thrown open and the stewardesses were thrown to the floor. Talk about having my heart in my mouth!

On another day, we'd had a perfect three-hour flight until we were diverted at the last moment. What made things worse was that I was sitting next to a window and knew the reason why we couldn't land at our intended destination. Seeing the wreckage of a crashed two-seater plane on the runway below us didn't exactly fill me with confidence as the pilot told us we'd be in the air for another hour. The drama didn't stop there either, because the next 60 minutes was like riding a roller-coaster at Blackpool as we caught alternate wafts of hot and cold thermals.

I'll never forget the forked lightning that made our night-flight to Aberdeen, with City, seem like a daytime experience. On one pre-season trip to Sweden, money must have been tight because we flew on the 'Paper Plane'. That wasn't what it was made from, although at times it felt like it, as we were seemingly tossed around by the gale-force winds. The Paper Plane got its name because it doubled up as a newspaper delivery service.

When we landed somewhere en route to Scandinavia, we begged Malcolm Allison to let us continue the journey by train, as we were feeling more than a little queasy as a result of the turbulence. He made us carry on the journey by air and I'll never forget the thunderous applause when we landed at our destination. The clapping and cheering was due to the relief we all felt rather than any particular admiration for the crew.

Mind you, the edge was taken off our feverish handclapping when the pilot calmly announced, 'Hope you enjoyed the extra part of the flight I added on at the end. I spent the last ten minutes swooping and circling as we descended so that you could all get a great view of the fantastic Swedish countryside below us. Hope you enjoyed the flight and will fly with us again soon!' We returned by train, though in all honesty that had always been the plan, for some reason.

I wouldn't swap my memories of playing football for anything. I'll admit that, as time has gone on, I've forgotten many of the details of individual games but I'll never forget the great players I competed with and against. I met up with several of them again during 2005 when I was inducted into the National Football Museum Hall of Fame.

Naturally, I would have preferred to have played on into my 30s but I enjoyed and achieved more during my slightly shortened career than most, and for that I'll always be grateful. I've never lost sight of my roots and will never forget the sacrifices my family made for me when I was a boy.

My favourite film is *Billy Elliot*, the story of a miner's son from the North-east who breaks the mould and becomes successful in his chosen field of ballet. I see many parallels between his story and my own life. When I watch the film, I'm taken back to my childhood.

My father was tough and hid his feelings, just as Billy's did, and I feel that I also broke the mould. I always believed in my ability, despite a certain amount of scepticism that I could make a career from my football talents.

I wish my father had still been here when I received the letter informing me that I was to be awarded the MBE in the New Year's Honours list, published on 1 January 2005. It was totally unexpected. The medal was given to me for my charity and community work, although I suspect my football career was a contributing factor.

It might have seemed appropriate to see the stage version of *Billy Elliot* in the West End when I made the trip to Buckingham Palace but I had other plans for the evening after the presentation. I was joined by Marie, Dawn and Jon on 27 April 2005 for the special occasion.

Naturally, I had to look my best for the ceremony, so I wore top hat and tails with Marie wearing a black outfit, complete with black and white hat. We stayed at a hotel close to Buckingham Palace, just a short walk from Dawn's Westminster flat. I had no idea who would be presenting the medal but I hoped it would be the Queen.

As a small boy, I remember going to Castle Eden to stand on the route where she would pass on her way to an important engagement in the area. Simply seeing her give the royal wave from the limousine window had been exciting enough. Now I was probably going to meet her face to face.

I'd met her daughter, Princess Anne, before the 1969 FA Cup final, as both teams were introduced to the royal party. That had been a great honour itself but this was taking it to a different level.

I slept well the night before, rising at about eight o'clock and leaving for the Palace at ten o'clock. There was a light breeze and I was worried that Marie's hat might be blown away. We entered through the main gates at the front of Buckingham Palace, the same entrance that I'd seen many times before being used by heads of state or for the Changing of the Guard.

Once inside the Palace, we were ushered up to the first floor. I was separated from Marie, Dawn and Jon as they went into the main hall. I was taken into a side room, where I was briefed about the etiquette on meeting Her Majesty. Now I knew for certain that it would be the Queen.

Other recipients that day included Ellen MacArthur, who was made a Dame, and Private Johnson Beharry, who received the Victoria Cross for his actions in Iraq. I felt very humble being in the company of such deserving individuals. Before Private Beharry received his VC, a citation was read to explain the two acts of bravery for which he was being recognised.

Among the words that were used to explain his heroism were, 'For his repeated extreme gallantry and unquestioned valour, despite intense direct attacks, personal injury and damage to his vehicle in the face of relentless enemy action, Private Beharry deserves the highest possible recognition.'

I could feel myself becoming quite emotional as the words were read. We had been told it was against protocol to applaud but I certainly felt like cheering this young man, whose achievements made mine seem insignificant by comparison.

When it was my turn to step forward, I proudly received my MBE from the Queen, who asked why I was receiving the award. I explained that it was for the charity work I had done as a former footballer. She smiled very kindly in a way that reminded me of my 'Mum'. I'd always thought Aunt Ella looked like the Queen and now I had seen them both in person, I couldn't help thinking that there was a remarkable resemblance. As the ceremony concluded, she walked down the centre aisle and seemed to smile at me as she walked past.

When I was reunited with Marie, Dawn and Jon, we had a few moments to mingle with the other guests. Marie and Jon immediately headed towards Private Beharry to congratulate him and to look at his VC, which Jon later explained to me was made from part of a cannon used in the Crimean War. He described it as looking rusty and very old but there's no doubt it is extremely special. By contrast, my MBE was shiny and new.

After formal and press photographs, we exited through the main gates into the real world. Tourists were standing six deep, having just watched the Changing of the Guard. An American couple asked me what had been going on, so I showed them my MBE and they responded enthusiastically.

Once we'd changed back into 'normal clothes', the rest of the day was spent celebrating, with Dawn buying dinner at L'Escargot in Soho. I don't think I've seen my MBE since. I'm sure Jon has slept with it around his neck with great pride.

I feel that I have been very lucky to have lived such a wonderful life. My football career and home circumstances could not have been better. I still enjoy a great relationship with football supporters all over the world but particularly the magnificent fans of *my* club, Manchester City.

We finished the day in London, by going to a West End show. One day I'm sure I'll watch the stage show of *Billy Elliot* but on this occasion we went to the Dominion Theatre to see the Ben Elton and Queen musical *We Will Rock You*. It was the perfect end to a perfect day.

As I sat there in the theatre, I couldn't help thinking to myself that I'd waited all my life to see the Queen, only to see *the* Queen twice in one day!

EPILOGUE
Extra Time

It was a very proud moment when I received my copy of the hardback version of *Reluctant Hero* in October 2005. I was pleased with the way it looked, and my friends, who had a sneak preview, all told me that they'd really enjoyed it.

My collaborator, Ian Cheeseman, advised me that we'd need to organise a book launch, the thought of which made me feel a little uneasy. I didn't fancy an event at which I would have to speak to businessmen and the media, so we decided that we'd make sure that most of those in attendance were ordinary Manchester City supporters. The launch was therefore staged at the City Social, which is located above the superstore at the City of Manchester Stadium. The audience was made up of grassroots fans who'd won tickets through the *Manchester Evening News*, BBC GMR and the City website.

Naturally, there were a few members of the press there, too, but Ian organised proceedings in a way that meant I didn't worry about it too much beforehand. The event passed by in such a whirl that it was over before I knew it.

While I was away on a short family holiday, Ian organised a tour of the Supporters Club branches that meant we were out virtually every evening from late November until Christmas. In addition to the visits to the branches, at which I answered questions and signed copies of the book, I also attended formal book-signing sessions all over the place and was asked to return to several of the bookshops to do additional signings behind the scenes. By the time Christmas arrived, I had to concentrate when signing, for fear that I might spell my own, rather simple name, incorrectly! I thoroughly enjoyed it all, though, and the supporters made me feel very welcome. I always appreciate the affection which they show towards me.

I don't think I realised how exhausting the whole process had been until it was over. We'd been on the road for about five weeks, and it must have taken just as long into the New Year before I felt like I was back in my old routine. The only way I can describe it is that it felt like I had jet lag!

As time progressed, more and more supporters came up to me and said they'd read the book and really enjoyed it. The number of people who've done that has astounded me. I believe it's just a simple life-story, and yet so many people have said that they think it is something special. People still talk to me about City and football related issues, of course, but I am pleased that they've taken time to read the book.

There is one person, though, that I am particularly grateful to for taking the time to read it. His name is Jim Hill, or, to give him his full title, Mr James Hill, Consultant General and Colorectal Surgeon.

Just as things seemed to have returned to normal in February 2006, my son Jon, who is a trainee in surgery, returned from the Manchester Royal Infirmary with a worried look on his face. It seems that a friend of Jon's called Doug Speake, a research fellow, had given a copy of my book to Jim Hill for Christmas.

Jim apparently enjoyed the book and had been particularly interested in the early chapters about my childhood. He had specifically noted the section about my birth mother dying at a young age. He casually asked Jon if he knew about the details of my mother's illness, which I'd described as a 'growth of the back body', and how it could possibly affect *me*. He explained that it could have been a reference to bowel cancer, and he recommended that I should look into it further as I might need to be checked over.

Jon was clearly concerned following his conservation with Jim, but *my* immediate reaction was that I was feeling fit and well, and that there was nothing to suggest that I could have anything wrong with me. Jon's reaction was, 'Never mind how you feel, you need to be examined.' He wouldn't let it rest.

I couldn't decide whether to have any tests or not, but in the end, just to keep Jon quiet and for peace of mind, I agreed. From that moment onwards, events seemed to take on a life of their own. Mr Hill recommended that he arrange a 'camera test' as quickly as possible, and all of a sudden an appointment had been made for Wednesday, 8 March. I was booked in to have a colonoscopy in the Endoscopy Unit at the Royal. It had originally been scheduled for the Monday, but City had a game against Sunderland the day before, and I'd had a long-standing arrangement to go out for a meal with friends on the Saturday evening, so I wasn't keen on having to starve myself on those days, ahead of the scope. Of course, I didn't really understand the urgency of the situation, so it was in a very matter-of-fact way that I'd suggested the appointment be put back. I thought that might delay things by a few weeks, but it was rearranged for just two days later!

A colonoscopy involves passing a fibre-optic instrument up your back passage, so, of course, it's essential that there's nothing in there when this happens! I therefore had to go through the process of starving myself to 'flush out the system'. What an experience that was! I'd walk into the kitchen, knowing I couldn't eat anything, looking enviously at the food in the dog's bowl. The thought of eating Pedigree Chum wouldn't normally make my mouth water, but I swear I'd have joined our dog Henry for a meal if the hunger pains had got any worse. I'm not a big eater, but I do enjoy my food little and often.

The other aspect of the cleansing process is taking a strong laxative to clear out the system. It was like dynamite, and I had to be within a few yards of a toilet at all times. Need I say more?

I met Mr Hill at the Royal on the Wednesday, and he told me that I could watch everything he was doing on a monitor in front of me, explaining that some patients felt it was helpful to see what was going on. He gave me an injection in the back of my hand while he was chatting to me, and I can't remember anything else that happened! I was out like a light and couldn't have watched the monitor, even if I'd wanted to. Of course, Marie was there through it all, at my side as usual.

Afterwards, we sat down to discuss his findings, though, to be honest, I was still doped up from the sedation, so I didn't say a word and left all the talking to Marie. However, his basic message was simple: he told us there was nothing to worry about, so we went home.

Once I was fully alert again, Marie told me that he'd said there might need to be a follow-up operation. Mr Hill had found some polyps inside my bowel. Apparently, there are two types of polyps: some that are described as 'looking like mushrooms', with a stem and a head, and some that grow like a carpet on the wall of the bowel. The 'mushroom polyps' can be removed straightforwardly during the colonoscopy, using a small instrument to lasso them and slice off the potentially harmful top. The other type are more difficult to remove, hence the reason for an operation.

When we saw Mr Hill the following week, he had the results of biopsies that he had taken during the colonoscopy, and he told me that an operation would be required. I casually suggested that it might be best to plan it for October; after all, he'd said that there was no reason to panic, and I felt fit and well. I'd come to this conclusion after carefully going through my summer holiday plans and City's fixture list. I thought the autumn would be a good time to have to spend indoors recovering from the surgery.

His reply was that while there was indeed no reason to panic, he wouldn't want to leave things until then. My face dropped. In a state of shock, I asked him when he thought the operation should be done, and he suggested the following Monday when he had an available slot. That was only a few days away!

Everything was happening so quickly; it had only been three or four weeks earlier that Jon had told me Mr Hill had read my book, and now I was facing a major operation. It was a shock. As I sat there in disbelief, he told me that the problem I had was like a time bomb waiting to go off. He said that he couldn't be certain if it would take six months, a year or five years before the growth turned fully cancerous, but he insisted that the quicker it was removed the better.

As shocked as I was, I don't think it really occurred to me at the time that I was coming face to face with my own mortality. Everything was happening so fast that it never really had time to sink in.

I was admitted to BUPA Hospital Manchester on Sunday, 19 March, and had the operation the following day. I spent two days in intensive care and was discharged home from the ward after a week, going home on the Saturday. At this point, I'll let Mr Hill take over the story:

> I found that on the right side of Colin's colon he had a four centimetre long, benign (fortunately) polyp growing on the bowel wall. It was the sort of growth that if left would almost certainly have developed into cancer. Depending on family history, that type of thing can progress quite quickly. His surgery was straightforward, he made a good recovery and the long-term consequences of having part of his bowel removed are minimal.
>
> I must admit, it did feel a bit surreal operating on Colin. In practical terms, it's no different to working on anyone else, because you always take the same level of care and attention, but he was a boyhood hero of mine. I'm a Huddersfield Town fan by birth, first becoming aware of football during the 1970 World Cup.
>
> I remember collecting silver Texaco coins, and, of course, I had one of Colin. I even remember sleeping in a light-blue Manchester City kit as a child when we were on a family holiday in the Lake District. I certainly can't get any pleasure out of watching United, but I do love watching City. To have played a part in extending the life of Colin Bell has been a privilege.

Once back at home, I knew it would be weeks before I would be back to normal. I couldn't do much in the first few days, and I wasn't allowed to lift things for quite a while, but I slowly returned to how I'd been before the operation. I missed a couple of City home games, primarily because I felt so uncomfortable sitting in one position for any length of time, but it was also obvious that I wasn't able to move normally, and I couldn't face the prospect of having to tell everyone about the experience I had gone through. My priority was to get back to full fitness, and then I would find the right time to tell people.

It's only now, with the problem sorted out, that everything that has happened has started to sink in. Just like before, I feel fit and healthy, but the reality is that I could have died from bowel cancer soon after my 60th birthday.

As a result of my experience, I now want to make as many people as possible think about their own circumstances and family trees. I've read about similar stories in the newspapers and seen recent TV programmes in which celebrities research their family history. They look into where they were born and trace the history of their ancestors. Having gone through what I've been through, I've come to the conclusion that looking into the health of family members should go hand in hand with researching your family tree. It doesn't matter whether it's your lungs, heart or whatever, it seems that some of the illnesses that you can suffer from are programmed into your genes. This sort of information should be passed down the line so that everyone who could be affected, in future generations, is aware of it.

Mr Hill tells me that the lifetime risk of developing bowel cancer is one in twenty. It's the third-most-common cancer in the UK – 16,000 people die from it each year. Screening for blood in stool samples is to be introduced nationally in 2006, which could reduce bowel cancer mortality by 15–33 per cent.

My former England teammate Bobby Moore died of the disease in 1993 at the age of just 51. If he'd been as lucky as me and been aware of the problem a couple of years earlier, he might have still been alive today. We'll never know for sure, of course, but if there had been a family history of the problem and he'd been aware of it, things might have been different.

I've been given the all-clear by Mr Hill, but I will have to go back to him for another check-up in two or three years' time. He tells me that if there are any new growths then, they will be the mushroom type, and he'll be able to remove them during a colonoscopy without the need for another major operation.

My sister Eileen is aware of what has happened; however, I don't know whether she is keen to have anything done at her age. My nephew Keith is naturally concerned as he's now in his 50s. He has decided to have a colonoscopy to look for any polyps that might otherwise progress to cancer if left *in situ*. He appears to be fit and well, but what's happened has certainly scared him.

It's the same with Jon and Dawn, although at this stage there isn't quite the same urgency because they're so much younger. I think that the fact this incident has scared them is good, and it's made them more aware of these issues.

There are always risks associated with any type of operation, but if your life's on the line, then there can be no choice. The things that doctors can do these days are fantastic. I must admit, I enjoy watching TV programmes about operations and that kind of thing. There are so many good surgeons around these days that I would tell people to just get on with it.

As I've discovered, bowel cancer can be prevented or cured. More than half of all patients, including those diagnosed as a result of rectal bleeding or loose bowel movements over a period of more than six weeks, make a full recovery. The earlier the problem is diagnosed, the higher the success rate.

My advice is, don't be embarrassed about your symptoms, and don't be embarrassed about the intrusive nature of the examination and possible treatment you might have to face. If I can do it, so can you!

Hopefully my life has been extended by a fair few years. I've got a smile on my face again after a few months of anxiety. Before the book was published, I was hoping to live into my 80s or 90s, but I now know that wouldn't have been the case.

My life has had a few twists and turns along the way. I believe everything happens for a reason, though. The knee injury that prematurely ended my playing days was meant to be. The setback I suffered at my trial with Arsenal, and the rejection of other clubs, led me to Bury and then Manchester City. I wouldn't change a thing. To have had the career I had and the family I have makes me believe I am a very lucky person. Someone up there likes me, and I believe they have been steering me through my life.

I'm now into 'extra time'. I've always been known for my stamina. These days I can't deny that my legs might struggle to carry me through this particular period of extra time – after all, my knees are not in the best of condition – but hopefully my heart and lungs will see me through. I'm not sure I'd want to take a penalty, though, if I get all the way through this particular period of extra time – unless, of course, it was a matter of life and death.

If you want more information about bowel cancer, contact the Bobby Moore Foundation at Cancer Research UK. Their website address is: http://www.cancerresearchuk.org/bobbymoorefund/bowelcancer/

APPENDIX

Summary of Career While at Manchester City

Appearances in All Competitions and Goals Scored

Competition	Appearances (as sub)	Goals
League	393 (+1)	117
FA Cup	33 (+1)	9
FL Cup	40	18
Europe	25 (+1)	8
Domestic	7	1
Reserves	60	12
International	45 (+3)	9
Representative	12	2
Total	615 (+5)	176

League Appearances and Goals Scored

Date	Venue	Opponents	Score	Goals
1965–66				
19 Mar	A	Derby County	2–1	1
2 Apr	H	Plymouth Argyle	1–1	
8 Apr	H	Bury	1–0	
12 Apr	A	Bury	1–2	
16 Apr	H	Bolton Wanderers	4–1	
23 Apr	A	Ipswich Town	1–1	
30 Apr	H	Birmingham City	3–1	1
4 May	A	Rotherham United	1–0	1
7 May		Leyton Orient	2–2	1
13 May	A	Charlton Athletic	3–2	
18 May	H	Southampton	0–0	
1966–67				
20 Aug	A	Southampton	1–1	
24 Aug	H	Liverpool	2–1	1
27 Aug	H	Sunderland	1–0	
30 Aug	A	Liverpool	2–3	
3 Sep	A	Aston Villa	0–3	
7 Sep	H	West Ham United	1–4	1
10 Sep	H	Arsenal	1–1	
17 Sep	A	Manchester United	0–1	
24 Sep	A	Blackpool	1–0	
1 Oct	H	Chelsea	1–4	
8 Oct	H	Tottenham Hotspur	1–2	
15 Oct	A	Manchester United	0–2	
29 Oct	A	Burnley	3–2	1
15 Nov	A	Newcastle United	0–2	
12 Nov	A	Stoke City	1–0	
19 Nov	H	Everton	1–0	1
26 Nov	A	Fulham	1–4	
3 Dec	H	Nottingham Forest	1–1	
10 Dec	A	West Bromwich Albion	1–3	
17 Dec	H	Southampton	1–1	1
27 Dec	A	Sheffield Wednesday	0–1	

1966–67

31 Dec	A	Sunderland	0–1	
2 Jan	H	Sheffield Wednesday	0–0	
14 Jan	A	Arsenal	0–1	
21 Jan	H	Manchester United	1–1	
4 Feb	H	Blackpool	1–0	1
11 Feb	A	Chelsea	0–0	
25 Feb	A	Tottenham Hotspur	1–1	
4 Mar	H	Burnley	1–0	1
18 Mar	A	Leeds United	0–0	
24 Mar	H	Leicester City	1–3	
25 Mar	H	West Bromwich Albion	2–2	
28 Mar	A	Leicester City	1–2	
1 Apr	A	Sheffield United	0–1	
12 Apr	H	Stoke City	3–1	3
19 Apr	H	Aston Villa	1–1	
22 Apr	H	Fulham	3–0	1
29 Apr	A	Everton	1–1	
2 May	A	Nottingham Forest	0–2	
6 May	H	Sheffield United	1–1	
8 May	H	Leeds United	2–1	
13 May	A	West Ham United	1–1	1

1967–68

19 Aug	H	Liverpool	0–0	
23 Aug	A	Southampton	2–3	1
26 Aug	A	Stoke City	0–3	
30 Aug	H	Southampton	4–2	2
2 Sep	H	Nottingham Forest	2–0	
6 Sep	H	Newcastle United	2–0	
9 Sep	A	Coventry City	3–0	1
16 Sep	H	Sheffield United	5–2	1
23 Sep	A	Arsenal	0–1	
30 Sep	H	Manchester United	1–2	1
7 Oct	A	Sunderland	0–1	
14 Oct	H	Wolverhampton Wanderers	2–0	
21 Oct	A	Fulham	4–2	
28 Oct	H	Leeds United	1–0	1

1967–68

4 Nov	A	Everton	1–1	
11 Nov	H	Leicester City	6–0	
18 Nov	A	West Ham United	3–2	
25 Nov	H	Burnley	4–2	
2 Dec	A	Sheffield Wednesday	1–1	
9 Dec	H	Tottenham Hotspur	4–1	1
16 Dec	A	Liverpool	1–1	
23 Dec	H	Stoke City	4–2	
20 Jan	A	Sheffield United	3–0	1
3 Feb	H	Arsenal	1–1	
24 Feb	H	Sunderland	1–0	
2 Mar	A	Burnley	1–0	
9 Mar	H	Coventry City	3–1	1
16 Mar	H	Fulham	5–1	1
23 Mar	A	Leeds United	0–2	
27 Mar	A	Manchester United	3–1	1
20 Apr	A	Wolverhampton Wanderers	0–0	
25 Apr	H	Sheffield Wednesday	1–0	
29 Apr	H	Everton	2–0	
4 May	A	Tottenham Hotspur	3–1	2
11 May	A	Newcastle United	4–3	

1968–69

10 Aug	A	Liverpool	1–2	
14 Aug	H	Wolverhampton Wanderers	3–2	
17 Aug	H	Manchester United	0–0	
21 Aug	A	Leicester City	0–3	
24 Aug	A	Queens Park Rangers	1–1	
27 Aug	A	Arsenal	1–4	1
31 Aug	H	Ipswich Town	1–1	1
7 Sep	A	Stoke City	0–1	
14 Sep	H	Southampton	1–1	
21 Sep	A	Sunderland	4–1	1
28 Sep	H	Leeds United	3–1	2
5 Oct	A	Everton	0–2	
9 Oct	H	Arsenal	1–1	1
12 Oct	H	Tottenham Hotspur	4–1	

1968–69

19 Oct	A	Coventry City	1–1	
26 Oct	H	Nottingham Forest	3–3	1
2 Nov	A	Chelsea	0–2	
9 Nov	H	Sheffield Wednesday	0–1	
16 Nov	A	Newcastle United	0–1	
23 Nov	H	West Bromwich Albion	5–1	2
30 Nov	A	West Ham United	1–2	
7 Dec	H	Burnley	7–0	2
14 Dec	A	Tottenham Hotspur	1–1	
21 Dec	H	Coventry City	4–2	
26 Dec	H	Everton	1–3	1
11 Jan	H	Chelsea	4–1	
4 Mar	A	Burnley	1–2	1
8 Mar	A	Manchester United	1–0	
15 Mar	H	Queens Park Rangers	3–1	
24 Mar	A	Nottingham Forest	0–1	
29 Mar	H	Stoke City	3–1	1
4 Apr	H	Leicester City	2–0	
5 Apr	A	Leeds United	0–1	
8 Apr	A	Wolverhampton Wanderers	1–3	
12 Apr	H	Sunderland	1–0	
16 Apr	A	West Bromwich Albion	0–2	
19 Apr	A	Southampton	0–3	
30 Apr	H	West Ham United	1–1	
12 May	H	Liverpool	1–0	

1969–70

9 Aug	H	Sheffield Wednesday	4–1	1
12 Aug	A	Liverpool	2–3	
16 Aug	A	Newcastle United	0–1	
20 Aug	H	Liverpool	0–2	
27 Aug	A	Sunderland	4–0	1
30 Aug	A	Burnley	1–1	
6 Sep	H	Chelsea	0–0	
13 Sep	A	Tottenham Hotspur	3–0	1
20 Sep	H	Coventry City	3–1	2
4 Oct	H	West Bromwich Albion	2–1	1

1969–70

Date	H/A	Opponent	Score	Goals
8 Oct	H	Newcastle United	2–1	
11 Oct	A	Nottingham Forest	2–2	
18 Oct	A	Derby County	1–0	
25 Oct	H	Wolverhampton Wanderers	1–0	
1 Nov	A	Ipswich Town	1–1	
8 Nov	H	Southampton	1–0	1
15 Nov	H	Manchester United	4–0	2
22 Nov	A	Arsenal	1–1	
29 Nov	H	Leeds United	1–2	
6 Dec	A	West Ham United	4–0	
6 Jan	H	Burnley	1–1	
10 Jan	A	Coventry City	0–3	
17 Jan	H	Stoke City	0–1	
31 Jan	A	West Bromwich Albion	0–3	
7 Feb	H	Nottingham Forest	1–1	
18 Feb	H	Arsenal	1–1	
21 Feb	A	Wolverhampton Wanderers	3–1	1
28 Feb	H	Ipswich Town	1–0	
11 Mar	H	Crystal Palace	0–1	
8 Apr	A	Southampton	0–0	
18 Apr	A	Leeds United	3–1	1

1970–71

Date	H/A	Opponent	Score	Goals
13 Aug	A	Southampton	1–1	1
19 Aug	A	Crystal Palace	1–0	
22 Aug	H	Burnley	0–0	
26 Aug	H	Blackpool	2–0	1
29 Aug	A	Everton	1–0	1
5 Sep	H	West Bromwich Albion	4–1	2
12 Sep	A	Nottingham Forest	1–0	
19 Sep	H	Stoke City	4–1	
26 Sep	A	Tottenham Hotspur	0–2	
3 Oct	H	Newcastle United	1–1	
10 Oct	A	Chelsea	1–1	1
17 Oct	H	Southampton	1–1	
24 Oct	A	Wolverhampton Wanderers	0–3	
31 Oct	H	Ipswich Town	2–0	1

1970–71

7 Nov	A	Coventry City	1–2	1
14 Nov	H	Derby County	1–1	1
21 Nov	H	West Ham United	2–0	
28 Nov	A	Leeds United	0–1	
5 Dec	H	Arsenal	0–2	
12 Dec	A	Manchester United	4–1	
19 Dec	A	Burnley	4–0	2
26 Dec	H	Huddersfield Town	1–1	1
9 Jan	H	Crystal Palace	1–0	
12 Jan	A	Liverpool	0–0	
16 Jan	A	Blackpool	3–3	1
30 Jan	H	Leeds United	0–2	
6 Feb	A	Arsenal	0–1	
13 Mar	A	Derby County	0–0	
20 Mar	H	Coventry City	1–1	
27 Mar	A	West Bromwich Albion	0–0	
3 Apr	H	Everton	3–0	
9 Apr	H	Nottingham Forest	1–3	
10 Apr	A	Huddersfield Town	0–1	
12 Apr	A	Newcastle United	0–0	

1971–72

28 Aug	H	Tottenham Hotspur	4–0	1
1 Sep	H	Liverpool	1–0	
4 Sep	A	Leicester City	0–0	
11 Sep	H	Manchester United	2–1	1
18 Sep	A	Nottingham Forest	2–2	
25 Sep	H	Southampton	3–0	1
23 Oct	H	Sheffield United	2–1	
30 Oct	A	Huddersfield town	1–1	
6 Nov	H	Manchester United	3–3	1
13 Nov	A	Arsenal	2–1	1
20 Nov	A	West Ham United	2–0	
27 Nov	H	Coventry City	4–0	2
4 Dec	A	Derby County	1–3	
11 Dec	H	Ipswich Town	4–0	1
18 Dec	H	Leicester City	1–1	

1971–72

Date	H/A	Opponent	Score	
27 Dec	A	Stoke City	3–1	
1 Jan	H	Nottingham Forest	2–2	
8 Jan	A	Tottenham Hotspur	1–1	
22 Jan	A	Crystal Palace	2–1	
29 Jan	H	Wolverhampton Wanderers	5–2	
12 Feb	A	Sheffield United	3–3	1
1 Mar	H	West Bromwich Albion	2–1	2
4 Mar	H	Arsenal	2–0	
11 Mar	A	Everton	2–1	
18 Mar	H	Chelsea	1–0	
25 Mar	A	Newcastle United	0–0	
1 Apr	H	Stoke City	1–2	
4 Apr	A	Southampton	0–2	
8 Apr	H	West Ham United	3–1	1
12 Apr	A	Manchester United	3–1	
15 Apr	A	Coventry City	1–1	
18 Apr	A	Ipswich Town	1–2	
22 Apr	H	Derby County	2–0	

1972–73

Date	H/A	Opponent	Score	
12 Aug	A	Liverpool	0–2	
16 Aug	H	Everton	0–1	
19 Aug	H	Norwich City	3–0	1
23 Aug	A	Derby County	0–1	
26 Aug	A	Chelsea	1–2	
29 Aug	H	Crystal Palace	0–1	
2 Sep	H	Leicester City	1–0	
9 Sep	A	Birmingham City	1–4	
16 Sep	H	Tottenham Hotspur	2–1	
23 Sep	A	Stoke City	1–5	
30 Sep	H	West Bromwich Albion	2–1	
7 Oct	H	Wolverhampton Wanderers	1–1	
14 Oct	A	Coventry City	2–3	
21 Oct	H	West Ham United	4–3	
28 Oct	A	Arsenal	0–0	
4 Nov	H	Derby County	4–0	1
11 Nov	A	Everton	3–2	

1972–73

Date		Opponent	Score	
18 Nov	H	Manchester United	3–0	2
25 Nov	A	Leeds United	0–3	
2 Dec	H	Ipswich Town	1–1	
9 Dec	A	Sheffield United	1–1	1
16 Dec	H	Southampton	2–1	
23 Dec	A	Newcastle United	1–2	
20 Jan	A	Leicester City	1–1	1
27 Jan	H	Birmingham City	1–0	
10 Feb	A	Tottenham Hotspur	3–2	
17 Feb	H	Liverpool	1–1	
3 Mar	A	Wolverhampton Wanderers	1–5	
6 Mar	A	Southampton	1–1	
10 Mar	H	Coventry City	1–2	
17 Mar	A	West Ham United	1–2	
24 Mar	H	Arsenal	1–2	
21 Mar	H	Leeds United	1–0	
7 Apr	A	Ipswich Town	1–1	
14 Apr	H	Sheffield United	3–1	1
18 Apr	H	Newcastle United	2–0	
21 Apr	A	Manchester United	0–0	
25 Apr	A	West Bromwich Albion	2–1	
28 Apr	H	Crystal Palace	2–3	

1973–74

Date		Opponent	Score	
25 Aug	H	Birmingham City	3–1	1
29 Aug	A	Derby County	0–1	
1 Sep	A	Stoke City	1–1	
5 Sep	H	Coventry City	1–0	
8 Sep	H	Norwich City	2–1	1
11 Sep	A	Coventry City	1–2	
15 Sep	A	Leicester City	1–1	1
22 Sep	H	Chelsea	3–2	
29 Sep	A	Burnley	0–3	
6 Oct	H	Southampton	1–1	
13 Oct	A	Newcastle United	0–1	
20 Oct	A	Sheffield United	2–1	
27 Oct	H	Leeds United	0–1	

1973–74

3 Nov	A	Wolverhampton Wanderers	0–0	
10 Nov	H	Arsenal	1–2	
17 Nov	H	Queens Park Rangers	1–0	
24 Nov	A	Ipswich Town	1–2	
8 Dec	A	West Ham United	1–2	
15 Dec	A	Tottenham Hotspur	2–0	1
22 Dec	H	Burnley	2–0	1
26 Dec	A	Everton	0–2	
29 Dec	A	Norwich City	1–1	
1 Jan	H	Stoke City	0–0	
12 Jan	H	Leicester City	2–0	
19 Jan	A	Birmingham City	1–1	
2 Feb	H	Tottenham Hotspur	0–0	
6 Feb	H	Derby County	1–0	1
9 Feb	A	Chelsea	0–1	
23 Feb	A	Southampton	2–0	
9 Mar	A	Leeds United	0–1	
13 Mar	H	Manchester United	0–0	
16 Mar	H	Sheffield United	0–1	
23 Mar	A	Arsenal	0–2	
27 Mar	H	Newcastle United	2–1	
30 Mar	H	Wolverhampton Wanderers	1–1	
6 Apr	H	Ipswich Town	1–3	
9 Apr	A	Queens Park Rangers	0–3	
12 Apr	H	Liverpool	1–1	
16 Apr	A	Liverpool	0–4	
20 Apr	H	West Ham United	2–1	1
27 Apr	A	Manchester United	1–0	

1974–75

17 Aug	H	West Ham United	4–0	
21 Aug	H	Tottenham Hotspur	1–0	
24 Aug	A	Arsenal	0–4	
28 Aug	A	Tottenham Hotspur	2–1	1
31 Aug	H	Leeds United	2–1	1
7 Sep	A	Coventry City	2–2	
14 Sep	H	Liverpool	2–0	

1974–75

21 Sep	A	Middlesbrough	0–3	
24 Sep	A	Carlisle United	0–0	
28 Sep	H	Queens Park Rangers	1–0	
5 Oct	H	Chelsea	1–1	1
12 Oct	A	Burnley	1–2	
16 Oct	H	Arsenal	2–1	
19 Oct	H	Luton Town	1–0	
26 Oct	A	Ipswich Town	1–1	1
2 Nov	A	Everton	0–2	
9 Nov	H	Stoke City	1–0	
16 Nov	A	Birmingham City	0–4	
23 Nov	H	Leicester City	4–1	1
30 Nov	A	Newcastle United	1–2	
7 Dec	H	Sheffield United	3–2	1
14 Dec	A	West Ham United	0–0	
21 Dec	H	Wolverhampton Wanderers	0–0	
26 Dec	A	Liverpool	1–4	1
28 Dec	H	Derby County	1–2	1
11 Jan	A	Sheffield United	1–1	
18 Jan	H	Newcastle United	5–1	1
1 Feb	A	Stoke City	0–4	
8 Feb	H	Everton	2–1	1
22 Feb	H	Birmingham City	3–1	1
1 Mar	A	Leeds United	2–2	
8 Mar	A	Leicester City	0–1	
15 Mar	A	Queens Park Rangers	0–2	
19 Mar	H	Carlisle United	1–2	
22 Mar	H	Coventry City	1–0	
28 Mar	H	Middlesbrough	2–1	1
29 Mar	A	Wolverhampton Wanderers	0–1	
1 Apr	A	Derby County	1–1	1
12 Apr	A	Chelsea	1–0	
19 Apr	H	Burnley	2–0	1
23 Apr	H	Ipswich Town	1–1	1
26 Apr	A	Luton town	1–1	

1975–76

16 Aug	H	Norwich City	3–0	1
20 Aug	H	Leicester City	1–1	
23 Aug	A	Coventry City	0–2	
27 Aug	A	Aston Villa	0–1	
30 Aug	H	Newcastle United	4–0	
6 Sep	A	West Ham United	0–1	
13 Sep	H	Middlesbrough	4–0	
20 Sep	A	Derby County	0–1	
24 Sep	H	Stoke City	1–0	
27 Sep	H	Manchester United	2–2	
4 Oct	A	Arsenal	3–2	
11 Oct	H	Burnley	0–0	
18 Oct	A	Tottenham Hotspur	2–2	1
25 Oct	H	Ipswich Town	1–1	1
1 Nov	A	Sheffield United	2–2	
8 Nov	H	Birmingham City	2–0	2
10 Apr	H	Derby County	4–3	
17 Apr	A	Leeds United	1–2	1
19 Apr	H	Liverpool	0–3	
24 Apr	H	Arsenal	3–1	

1977–78

26 Dec	H	Newcastle United	4–0	Sub
27 Dec	A	Middlesbrough	2–0	
31 Dec	H	Aston Villa	2–0	
2 Jan	A	Leicester City	1–0	
14 Jan	H	West Ham United	3–2	
21 Jan	A	Norwich City	3–1	
11 Feb	H	Queens Park Rangers	2–1	1
17 Feb	A	Bristol City	2–2	
25 Feb	H	Everton	1–0	
4 Mar	A	Arsenal	0–3	
15 Mar	A	Manchester United	2–2	
18 Mar	A	Wolverhampton Wanderers	1–1	1
25 Mar	H	Middlesbrough	2–2	
22 Apr	A	Birmingham City	4–1	
25 Apr	H	Coventry City	3–1	

1977–78

29 Apr	H	Derby County	1–1
1 May	H	Liverpool	0–4

1978–79

11 Nov	H	Derby County	1–2
3 Feb	A	Tottenham Hotspur	3–0
10 Feb	H	Manchester United	0–3
21 Apr	H	Queens Park Rangers	3–1
24 Apr	H	Middlesbrough	1–0
28 Apr	A	Southampton	0–1
1 May	H	Birmingham City	3–1
5 May	H	Bristol City	2–0
9 May	A	Nottingham Forest	1–3
15 May	H	Aston Villa	2–3

FA Cup Appearances and Goals Scored

Date	Venue	Round (Replay)	Opponents	Score	Goals
1966–67					
28 Jan	H	3	Leicester City	2–1	
18 Feb	A	4	Cardiff City	1–1	
22 Feb	H	4(R)	Cardiff City	3–1	1
11 Mar	H	5	Ipswich Town	1–1	
14 Mar	A	5(R)	Ipswich Town	3–0	
8 Apr	A	6	Leeds United	0–1	
1967–68					
27 Jan	H	3	Reading	0–0	
31 Jan	A	3(R)	Reading	7–0	1
17 Feb	H	4	Leicester City	0–0	
19 Feb	A	4(R)	Leicester City	3–4	1
1968–69					
4 Jan	H	3	Luton Town	1–0	
24 Feb	A	5	Blackburn Rovers	4–1	
1 Mar	H	6	Tottenham Hotspur	1–0	
22 Mar	N	S	Everton	1–0	
26 Apr	W	F	Leicester City	1–0	

1969–70

3 Jan	A	3	Hull City	1–0	
24 Jan	A	4	Manchester United	0–1	

1970–71

2 Jan	H	3	Wigan Athletic	1–0	1
23 Jan	A	4	Chelsea	3–0	2
17 Feb	H	5	Arsenal	1–2	1

1971–72

15 Jan	H	3	Middlesbrough	1–1	
18 Jan	A	3(R)	Middlesbrough	0–1	

1972–73

13 Jan	H	3	Stoke City	3–2	1
3 Feb	A	4	Liverpool	0–0	
7 Feb	H	4(R)	Liverpool	2–0	1
24 Feb	H	5	Sunderland	2–2	
27 Feb	A	5(R)	Sunderland	1–3	

1973–74

5 Jan	A	3	Oxford United	5–2	
27 Jan	A	4	Nottingham Forest	1–4	

1974–75

4 Jan	A	3	Newcastle United	0–2	

(played Maine Road)

1977–78

7 Jan	A	3	Leeds United	2–1	
31 Jan	A	4	Nottingham Forest	1–2	

1978–79

15 Jan	H	3	Rotherham United	0–0	
27 Jan	A	4	Shrewsbury Town	0–2	Sub

Football League Cup Appearances and Goals Scored

Date	Venue	Round–Leg (Replay)	Opponents	Score	Goals
1966–67					
14 Sep	H	2	Bolton Wanderers	3–1	1

1966–67

5 Oct	A	3	West Bromwich Albion	2–4	

1967–68

13 Sep	H	2	Leicester City	4–0	
11 Oct	H	3	Blackpool	1–1	
18 Oct	A	3(R)	Blackpool	2–0	
1 Nov	A	4	Fulham	2–3	1

1968–69

5 Sep	A	2	Huddersfield Town	0–0	
11 Sep	H	2(R)	Huddersfield Town	4–0	1
25 Sep	A	3	Blackpool	0–1	

1969–70

3 Sep	A	2	Southport	3–0	1
24 Sep	H	3	Liverpool	3–2	
15 Oct	H	4	Everton	2–0	1
29 Oct	H	5	Queens Park Rangers	3–0	2
3 Dec	H	S–1	Manchester United	2–1	1
7 Mar	W	F	West Bromwich Albion	2–1	

1970–71

9 Sep	A	2	Carlisle United	1–2	

1971–72

8 Sep	H	2	Wolverhampton Wanderers	4–3	2

1972–73

6 Sep	H	2	Rochdale	4–0	1
3 Oct	A	3	Bury	0–2	

1973–74

2 Oct	A	2	Walsall	0–0	
22 Oct	H	2(R)	Walsall	0–0	
30 Oct	N	2(2nd R)	Walsall	4–0	1
6 Nov	A	3	Carlisle United	1–0	
21 Nov	A	4	York City	0–0	
5 Dec	H	4(R)	York City	4–1	
19 Dec	A	5	Coventry City	2–2	
16 Jan	H	5(R)	Coventry City	4–2	
23 Jan	A	S–1	Plymouth Argyle	1–1	
30 Jan	H	S–2	Plymouth Argyle	2–0	1

1973–74

2 Mar	W	F	Wolverhampton Wanderers	1–2	1

1974–75

10 Sep	H	2	Scunthorpe United	6–0	3
9 Oct	A	3	Manchester United	0–1	

1975–76

10 Sep	A	2	Norwich City	1–1	
17 Sep	H	2(R)	Norwich City	2–2	
29 Sep	N	2(2nd R)	Norwich City	6–1	
8 Oct	H	3	Nottingham Forest	2–1	1
12 Nov	H	4	Manchester United	4–0	

1977–78

18 Jan	H	5	Arsenal	0–0	
24 Jan	A	5(R)	Arsenal	0–1	

1978–79

12 Dec	A	5	Southampton	1–2	

Appearances in European Competitions and Goals Scored

Date	Venue	Round–Leg	Opponents	Score	Goals

European Cup

1968–69

18 Sep	H	1–1	Fenerbahçe	0–0	
2 Oct	A	1–2	Fenerbahçe	1–2	

European Cup-Winners' Cup

1969–70

17 Sep	A	1–1	Athletic Bilbao	3–3	
1 Oct	H	1–2	Athletic Bilbao	3–0	1
12 Nov	A	2–1	Lierse SK	3–0	1
26 Nov	H	2–2	Lierse SK	5–0	2
4 Mar	A	3–1	Academica de Coimbra	0–0	
18 Mar	H	3–2	Academica de Coimbra	1–0	
1 Apr	A	S–1	Schalke 04	0–1	
15 Apr	H	S–2	Schalke 04	5–1	1

1969–70

29 Apr	N	F	Gornik Zabrze	2–1	

1970–71

16 Sep	H	1–1	Linfield	1–0	1
30 Sep	A	1–2	Linfield	1–2	
31 Oct	A	2–1	Honved	1–0	
4 Nov	H	2–2	Honved	2–0	1
10 Mar	A	3–1	Gornik Zabrze	0–2	
24 Mar	H	3–2	Gornik Zabrze	2–0	
31 Mar	N	3(R)	Gornik Zabrze	3–1	

Anglo–Italian LCW Trophy

1970–71

2 Sep	A		Bologna	0–1
23 Sep	H		Bologna	2–2

UEFA Cup

1972–73

13 Sep	H	1–1	Valencia	2–2
27 Sep	A	1–2	Valencia	1–2

1978–79

27 Sep	H	1–2	FC Twente Enschede	3–2	1 Sub
18 Oct	H	2–1	Standard Liege	4–0	
1 Nov	A	2–2	Standard Liege	0–2	
23 Nov	A	3–1	AC Milan	2–2	

Appearances in Domestic Competitions and Goals Scored

Date	Venue	Opponents		Score	Goals
Charity Shield					
1968–69					
3 Aug	H	West Bromwich Albion		6–1	
1969–70					
2 Aug	A	Leeds United		1–2	1
1972–73					
5 Aug	A	Aston Villa		1–0	

1973–74

18 Aug	H	Burnley	0–1

Texaco Cup
1974–75

3 Aug	A	Blackpool	1–1
6 Aug	A	Sheffield United	2–4
10 Aug	H	Oldham Athletic	2–1

League Appearances for Manchester City Reserves and Goals Scored

Date	Venue	Opponents	Score	Goals
1975–76				
17 Jan	A	Blackpool	0–0	
6 Mar	A	Everton	1–1	
10 Mar	H	Leeds United	1–1	
13 Mar	H	Burnley	2–0	
20 Mar	A	Wolverhampton Wanderers	1–1	
1976–77				
30 Mar	H	Sheffield United	1–0	
2 Apr	H	Nottingham Forest	0–3	
5 Apr	A	Coventry City	0–1	
9 Apr	A	Preston North End	3–3	1
13 Apr	A	Bolton Wanderers	1–2	
16 Apr	A	Coventry City	2–0	
28 Apr	H	West Bromwich Albion	3–1	
30 Apr	H	Liverpool	1–1	
2 May	A	Blackpool	1–0	
4 May	H	Derby County	2–1	1
1977–78				
17 Sep	H	Huddersfield Town	2–1	
20 Sep	H	Stoke City	0–0	
24 Sep	A	Burnley	1–2	
1 Oct	H	Everton	0–0	
4 Oct	H	Leeds United	1–2	

1977–78

8 Oct	A	Sheffield United	5–0	1
11 Oct	H	Bury	0–0	
15 Oct	H	Nottingham Forest	4–0	
22 Oct	A	Bolton Wanderers	4–2	
5 Nov	H	West Bromwich Albion	4–0	1
8 Nov	A	Coventry City	4–1	
12 Nov	A	Liverpool	0–2	
19 Nov	H	Blackpool	3–1	
26 Nov	A	Blackburn Rovers	4–1	
3 Dec	H	Newcastle United	2–1	1
10 Dec	A	Derby County	2–0	
17 Dec	H	Sheffield Wednesday	4–1	
1 Apr	A	West Bromwich Albion	2–1	1
8 Apr	H	Blackburn Rovers	2–0	
11 Apr	A	Bury	2–2	
15 Apr	A	Blackpool	3–1	1
18 Apr	H	Liverpool	1–0	

1978–79

13 Aug	H	Aston Villa	4–1	1
23 Aug	A	Nottingham Forest	4–3	1
26 Aug	A	Blackpool	2–0	1
2 Sep	H	Liverpool	0–0	
5 Sep	A	Sheffield Wednesday	3–0	
9 Sep	A	Blackburn Rovers	3–2	
16 Sep	H	Leeds United	0–0	
19 Sep	H	Everton	1–0	
30 Sep	H	Manchester United	0–2	
3 Oct	A	Liverpool	0–2	
7 Oct	H	Coventry City	1–1	
21 Oct	H	Bolton Wanderers	1–1	1
28 Oct	A	West Bromwich Albion	0–0	
9 Dec	A	Bury	4–2	1
16 Dec	H	Burnley	4–1	
10 Mar	H	West Bromwich Albion	2–1	
13 Mar	H	Sheffield Wednesday	1–0	
21 Mar	H	Preston North End	3–0	

1978–79

24 Mar	H	Nottingham Forest	0–1
4 Apr	A	Sheffield United	2–2
10 Apr	H	Wolverhampton Wanderers	3–1
14 Apr	A	Everton	0–2
18 Apr	A	Wolverhampton Wanderers	0–0

England International Appearances and Goals Scored

Date	Opponents	Venue	Score	Tournament	Position	Goals
1967–68						
22 May	Sweden	Wembley	3–1	F	7	
1 Jun	West Germany	Hanover	0–1	F	8	
1968–69						
11 Dec	Bulgaria	Wembley	1–1	F	8	
12 Mar	France	Wembley	5–0	F	8	
7 May	Wales	Wembley	2–1	F	8	
8 Jun	Uruguay	Montevideo	2–1	F	8	
12 Jun	Brazil	Rio de Janeiro	1–2	F	8	1
1969–70						
5 Nov	Holland	Amsterdam	1–0	F	8	1
10 Dec	Portugal	Wembley	1–0	F	8	
14 Jan	Holland	Wembley	0–0	F	8	
21 Apr	Northern Ireland	Wembley	3–1	F	Sub	
7 Jun	Brazil	Guadalajara	0–1	WC	Sub	
11 Jun	Czechoslovakia	Guadalajara	1–0	WC	7	
14 Jun	West Germany	Leon	2–4	WC	Sub	
1971–72						
1 Dec	Greece	Athens	2–0	ECQ	4	
23 Apr	West Germany	Wembley	1–3	ECQ	4	
13 May	West Germany	Berlin	0–0	ECQ	8	
20 May	Wales	Ninian Park	3–0	F	8	1
23 May	Northern Ireland	Wembley (capt.)	0–1	F	8	
27 May	Scotland	Hampden Park	1–0	F	8	

1972–73

11 Oct	Yugoslavia	Wembley	1–1	F	10	
15 Nov	Wales	Ninian Park	1–0	WCQ	10	1
24 Jan	Wales	Wembley	1–1	WCQ	8	
14 Feb	Scotland	Hampden Park	5–0	F	4	
12 May	Northern Ireland	Goodison Park	2–1	F	4	
15 May	Wales	Wembley	3–0	F	4	
19 May	Scotland	Wembley	1–0	F	4	
27 May	Czechoslovakia	Prague	1–1	F	4	
6 Jun	Poland	Chorzow	0–2	WCQ	8	

1973–74

26 Sep	Austria	Wembley	7–0	F	4	1
17 Oct	Poland	Wembley	1–1	WCQ	4	
14 Nov	Italy	Wembley	0–1	F	4	
11 May	Wales	Ninian Park	2–0	F	8	
15 May	Northern Ireland	Wembley	1–0	F	10	
18 May	Scotland	Hampden Park	0–2	F	8	
22 May	Argentina	Wembley	2–2	F	6	
29 May	East Germany	Leipzig	1–1	F	10	
1 Jun	Bulgaria	Sofia	1–0	F	10	
5 Jun	Yugoslavia	Belgrade	2–2	F	10	

1974–75

30 Oct	Czechoslovakia	Wembley	3–0	ECQ	7	2
20 Nov	Portugal	Wembley	0–0	ECQ	7	
12 May	West Germany	Wembley	2–0	F	4	1
16 Apr	Cyprus	Wembley	5–0	ECQ	4	
11 May	Cyprus	Limassol	1–0	ECQ	4	
17 May	Northern Ireland	Windsor Park	0–0	F	4	
24 May	Scotland	Wembley	5–1	F	4	1

1975–76

3 Sep	Switzerland	Basle	2–1	F	11	
30 Oct	Czechoslovakia	Bratislava	1–2	ECQ	11	

Other Internationals or Representative Games and Goals Scored

Date	Opponents	Venue	Score	Position	Goals
Under-23					
1967–68					
7 Feb	Scotland	Hampden Park	2–1	7	
1 May	Hungary	Goodison Park	4–0	7	1
'B' Internationals					
1969–70					
20 May	Colombia	Bogotá	1–0	7	
24 May	Ecuador	Quinto	4–1	8	
Inter-League					
1967–68					
8 Nov	League of Ireland	Dalymount Park	7–2	11	
1968–69					
27 Nov	Irish League	Windsor Park	1–0	8	
1972–73					
27 May	Scottish League	Hampden Park	2–2	11	
1973–74					
20 Mar	Scottish League	Maine Road	5–0	8	1
Expo Tournament					
3 Jun	FA XI v. Mexico XI	Montreal	3–0		
11 Jun	FA XI v. West Germany XI	Montreal	3–2		
Representative					
1967–68					
17 May	England v. Young England	Highbury	1–4	7	
1968–69					
4 Jun	England v. Mexico XI	Guadalajara	4–0		